MEET CUTE STORY IDEAS FOR PARANORMAL ROMANCE

Creative Writing Prompts

KING & CARPENTER

STORYSPARK PRESS
· BY WRITERS · FOR WRITERS ·

Published by **Story Spark Press**

National Library of New Zealand Cataloguing-in-Publication Data
Meet Cute Story Ideas for Paranormal Romance / King & Carpenter
Softcover – 978-0-473-69197-4
ebook – 978-0-473-69198-1

Thank You!

& A Small Request...

Thank you so much for reading this collection of Meet Cutes and we hope it has sparked many Romance Stories Ideas. If you could **please post a review** on Amazon or Goodreads, we would really appreciate it.

All the best, Love,
King & Carpenter.

This Book Belongs To:

CONTENTS

How to Use This Book 7

***~ Academy ~* 10**

Familiar Face 10
Inappropriate Instalove 11
Instant Rivals 12
Knight or Squire? 13
Lab Partners 14
Loss of Control 15
Love Potion Accident 16
Roommates at War 17

***~ Aliens ~* 18**

Bartered Bride 18
Diplomat to the Alien King 19
Kidnapped Bride & the Warrior 20
Mail Order Bride & the Alien Rancher 21
Prize for the Alien Gladiator 22
Sanctuary With the Alien Monks 23
Seahorse Alien Daddy 24
Terraforming Tinder 25
War Trophy Wife 26

***~ Angels ~* 27**

Angel Training Dropout 27
Avenging Angel 28
Caught Out by a Clean Window 29
Dark Angels 30
Guardian Angel Blunder 31
Penthouse Hired Help 32
Warrior Angel 33

***~ Anomalies & Accidents ~* 34**

Body Swap 34
Body Swap Pet 35
Doctor, Doctor 36
Immaculate Conception 37
Invisible MC 38
Memory Issues 39
Mystery Disappearances 40
Portals 41
Secret World Beneath the Ice 42
Trapped in a Smart House 43

***~ Curses ~* 44**

Cursed Jewels and Heirlooms 44
Lying Mirror 45
Pandora's Box 46
Sleeping Beauty Twist 47
Unlucky In Love 48

***~ Deities ~* 49**

Deity in Human Skin 49
Half-Blood Deity 50
Hunky Heaven 51
Lesser Known Deity 52
Lonely Hearts Club 53
Poseidon 54

~ Demons and Devils ~ 55

Accidentally Summoned 55
Badder Than Bad 56
Betrothed to the Devil 57
Devil in Sheep's Clothing 58
Other Side of the Fence 59
The Devil is in the Details 60
Underworld Spouse 61
Unwilling Sacrifice 62
Working for the Devil 63

~ Dragons ~ 64

All That Glitters Is Not Gold 64
Baby Dragon Daycare 65
Competitive Runners 65
Captured Royal 66
Falling for the Thief 67
Into the Dragon's Den 68
MC With The Dragon Tattoo 69
Mistaken Thief 70
Need a Light? 71
Never Wake A Sleeping Dragon 72
Royal Dragon 73

~ Fae ~ 74

Betrothed to the Fae 74
Blue Cap Blues 75
Changeling 76
Fae in the Family 77
Falling for the Fairy Godmother 78

~ Game lit & litrPg ~ 79

AI NPC Spouse 79
Apocalyptic Adventurer 80
Dungeon Beast Harem Collector 81
Forever Farming 82
I Took an Arrow to the Knee 83
Immersive 'Player' Mansion 84
Player Two 85
Trapped in a Dating Sim 86

~ Ghosts ~ 87

Hearing Voices 87
I'll Wait For You 88
Incompetent Necromancer 89
It's in the Ectoplasm 90
Kiss of Death 91
Mistaken Killer 92
Near Death Experience 93
Second Chances Dating Agency 94
The Ghost That Didn't Know 95

~ Immortals ~ 96

Dance With Death 96
Dreaming of the Sandman 97
Elixir Of Life 98
Immortal Recognized 99
Immortal Hunter 100
Slept In 101

~Monsters & Mythical Creatures~ 102

Blind Date With A Beast 102
Genie in a Bottle 103
Meeting with Medusa 104
Phoenix and the Fireman 105
Siren Song 106

~ Portals & Teleportation ~ 107

Pocket Dimension Prison 107
Summoning/Banishing Mishap 108
Teleportation Mishap 109
Time Warp 110

~ Psychic Powers and Mind Magic ~ 111

Connected Conscious 111
Dreaming of You 112
Mind Swap 113
Telepathic Job Interview 114

~ Robots and Cyborgs ~ 115

Model Mix Up! 115
Steampunk Patchwork Hearts 116
Time Travel Cyborg 117

~ Shape Shifters ~ 118

Bare Naked 118
Hit and Run 119
Injured Bear 120
Mama Bear 121
Raven 122
Researcher 123
Shacking Up with Goldilocks 124
Shark! 125
Shelter from the Storm 126
Teddy Bear's Picnic 127

~ Soul Magic ~ 128

Blood Ties 128
Kiss of Life, Soul Mate Bind 129
Soul Mate Agency Duds 130

~ Superpowers ~ 131

Alone No Longer 131
Town with Secrets 132
Untouchable 133

~Time Travel & Time Manipulation~ 134

Apprentice 134
Gateway to the Past 135
Past meets Present 136
Rewind Time 137
Time Freeze 138

~ Vampires ~ 139

Brought to the Vampire Court 139
Failed Feeding 140
Failed Thrall 141
Meet Me at Midnight 142
Royal Vampire 143
Saved by Dinner 144
Saved by the Vampire 145
Vampire Mafia 146
Vegan Vampire 147
Your Friendly Neighbourhood Vamp 148

~ Werewolves ~ 149

Accidental Imprint 149
Date With The Vet (Beta/Omega) 150
Fated Mates/Imprinted Mates 151
First Date, Interrupted 152
Living With Wolves 153
My, What Big Teeth You Have 154
Teacher's Pet 155
Unwilling Imprint 156
Wolf Tamer 157

~ Werewolves & Vampires 158

Disagreeing With Destiny 158
Second Chance Proposal 159

~ Witches/Wizards ~ 160

Buying a Broomstick 160
Crash Landing! 161
Disloyal Familiar 162
Halloween Party 163
Ley With Me 164
Oven Coven 165
Scrying Mess Up 166
Soup Kitchen Christmas 167
Tangled Tarot Reading 168
Witch Way 169

~ Zodiac ~ 170

Cat's Revenge 170
Hidden Dragon 171
Injured Tiger 172
Kidnapped Zodiac Spouse 173
Mistaken Zodiac 174
Paranormal Matchmaker 175
Powerless Zodiac Guardian 176
Zodiac Heir 177
Zodiac Military 178

~ Writing Craft Section ~ 179

Understanding the Meet-Cute 179

Glossary of Classic Romance Tropes 181

Age Gap 181
Alpha 181
Billionaire 182
Bodyguard, and Military 182
Celebrity 183
Cinderella 183
Enemies to Lovers 184
Fake Dating 185
Fish-out-of-water 185
Forced Proximity 186
Friends to Lovers 186
Grumpy Sunshine 187
Instalove 188
Marriage of Convenience 188
Opposites Attract 189
Romantic Suspense 190
RomCom 191
Royalty / Social Elite 192
Second Chance Romance 193

Bonus Amplifier Questions 195

HOW TO USE THIS BOOK

Welcome fellow Romance Writer. Whether you're looking for the next idea for a novel, short story, or film script, we hope that the collections of creative writing prompts here will help spark your next—or your first—paranormal romance story.

All the prompts, meet-cute and story set-ups were devised by us, using our human brains, and as professional writers, we hope our experience and knowledge will help get your creative juices and ideas flowing.

There are just under one-hundred and seventy prompts, each grouped under a suggested paranormal category within the overarching category of Paranormal Romance.

The paranormal categories include: **Academy, Aliens, Angels, Anomalies and Accidents, Curses, Deities, Demons and Devils, Dragons, Fae, GameLit & LitRPG, Ghosts, Immortals, Monsters and Mythical Creatures, Portals and Teleportation, Psychic Powers and Mind Magic, Robots and Cyborgs, Shape Shifters, Soul Magic, Superpowers, Time Travel and Manipulation, Vampires, Werewolves, Witches/ Wizards**, and the **Zodiac.**

While these suggestions are based on genre expectations, we encourage mixing and matching. Whenever possible, take the time to stop and think about how you might subvert or reimagine each story prompt to create some truly unique ideas that only you will come up with.

This book assumes you are familiar with the term Meet-Cute and writing tropes commonly applied to any form of romance writing, paranormal or otherwise. Tropes, for example, such as Enemies to Lovers, or, Grumpy-Sunshine.

However, if these terms are unfamiliar, **you will find a Writing Craft section explaining what a meet-cute is, how to use it and why it's important**, at the back of the book on page 179.

Plus there's also a detailed **Glossary of Classic Romance Tropes**, clearly explaining what each trope represents to most readers. We have provided the core tropes that really form the backbone of the majority of romance stories regardless of subgenre.

The core classic tropes covered are: **Age Gap, Alpha, Billionaire, Bodyguard/Military, Celebrity, Cinderella, Enemies to Lovers, Fake Dating, Fish-out-of-water, Forced Proximity, Friends to Lovers, Grumpy Sunshine, Instalove, Marriage of Convenience, Opposites Attract, Romantic Suspense, RomCom, Royalty, Second Chance Romance.**

However, as there are many, many tropes beyond what we have listed here, be sure to do some research on your own. After each Meet-Cute idea we list complementary tropes and subgenres to get you started. Just remember, classics remain popular for a reason, so we suggest starting with a classic trope and layer it with additional tropes that complement your story.

Speaking of layering. Tucked at the back of the book is a bonus list of **Amplifier Questions** that will help you elevate any of the meet-cute and story ideas to the next level, by providing additional thoughts to consider. Asking yourself these questions will help you tweak a meet-cute setup concept and craft something that is truly unique to you and more to your liking and purpose.

We highly recommend you have pen and paper to hand to make your own notes, because while you can use each story prompt exactly as it's described, you will most likely find our ideas spark your own ideas. Don't let those original ideas disappear. Write them down!

Because romance stories traditionally involve two people, this basic convention has been followed for convenience only. To identify each character, they are abbreviated as **MC1** and **MC2** for **M**ain **C**haracter.

The only assumption made with the structure of each prompt is that **MC1 is the Point-of-View character** from which the scene will be written. But don't let that stop you. It's always a worthwhile exercise to consider how the scene dynamics would be impacted if the point of view character was swapped.

Genders, **ages**, and **ethnicities *are not* assumed** and the simple mental exercise of swapping around these defining factors, from whatever you first assumed, will greatly increase the chances of coming up with more than one story from a single starting idea.

Finally, through out this book, there are spaces to make your own notes, as below:

NOTES:

Got that pencil handy? Great! Let's begin!

THEME OR SUBGENRE

~ ACADEMY ~

FAMILIAR FACE

The Meet Cute setup: MC1's life is in turmoil. Still reeling from being dumped by their first love (MC2), and now they've developed 'weirdo' magical/special powers and are forced to go to a new school for people like them.

But maybe it's time to accept that they aren't 'normal'? Maybe by doing so they can finally move on from the past and find their future? At least in a new school no one will know of their humiliating past and break up!

The dream of a fresh start is shattered when MC1 trips over another student in the halls and looks up only to see MC2 staring back at them in surprise/horror.

Is this why they broke up? Was MC2 hiding secret powers all along?

And even if MC2 is still interested, can MC1 ever trust them again?

Suggested Paranormal Genre/Subgenre: Academy.

Suggested Classic Romance Trope(s): Second Chance Romance.

Complimentary Romance Tropes and Paranormal Subgenres: Curses, Dark Romance, Dragons, Fae, Fairytale Retelling, Fated Mates, Found Family, Harem/ Reverse Harem, LitRPG, Monster Romance, Mythical Creatures, Portal, Psychic Powers, Science-Fiction Romance, Seasonal, Secret Royalty, Shape Shifters, Soul Mates, Steampunk, Superpowers, Urban Fantasy, Vampires, Werewolves, Witches/ Wizards, Zodiac.

NOTES:

INAPPROPRIATE INSTALOVE

The Meet Cute setup: MC1 arrives at their new Academy but falls into Instalove with the worst possible person! Is MC2 the wrong magical species, a young hot teacher, most popular guy/girl, an outcast, or a cursed pariah?

Some helpful examples: Perhaps their families are sworn enemies just like Romeo and Juilet. They could be a student and teacher. Or possibly from enemy species such as Werewolves and Vampires or Demons and Angels. To make matters worse, why not combine all three: feuding families, student/teacher and enemy species!

How are they going to get past the societal, social, physical or ethical barriers to get their happy ending?

And what does MC2 think of MC1 in the beginning? Do they see them as an untrustworthy rival, student, abhorred social group or class? Maybe MC2 doesn't even notice poor smitten MC1...

Suggested Paranormal Genre/Subgenre: Academy.

Suggested Classic Romance Trope(s): Age Gap, Enemies To Lovers, Instalove, Opposites Attract.

Complimentary Romance Tropes and Paranormal Subgenres: Blind Date, Bully Romance, Christmas, Curses, Dark Romance, Deities, Demons and Devils, Destiny, Divine Intervention, Dragons, Fae, Fairytale Retelling, Fated Mates, Found Family, Ghosts, Harem/Reverse Harem, Historical, Immortals, Monster Romance, Mythical Creatures, Secret Royalty, Shape Shifters, Soul Mates, Steampunk, Superpowers, Time Travel, Urban Fantasy, Valentine's Day, Vampires, Werewolves, Witches/Wizards, Zodiac.

NOTES:

INSTANT RIVALS

The Meet Cute setup: When fellow students MC1 and MC2 meet, they get off on the wrong foot and immediately become rivals trying to outdo each other in every class. Perhaps this electric chemistry will develop into something stronger as they learn sometimes collaboration can be better than competition.

Considerations: What is at the heart of their misunderstanding? Basing the Meet-Cute around the creation point of their animosity will help drive the story, so choose it carefully. Could a third party–an older student or sibling–have given MC1 deliberately false information about MC2? Maybe MC2 caught MC1 rifling through their bag or locker?

In addition, combining a misunderstanding along with both characters possessing the same win-at-all-costs attitude will amplify their desire to succeed above everything and everyone.

Suggested Paranormal Genre/Subgenre: Academy.

Suggested Classic Romance Trope(s): Enemies to Lovers.

Complimentary Romance Tropes and Paranormal Subgenres: Academy, Action and Adventure, Bully Romance, Dark Romance, Deities, Demons and Devils, Destiny, Divine Intervention, Dragons, Fae, Fairytale Retelling, Fated Mates, Found Family, GameLit, Genie in a Bottle, Ghosts, Harem/Reverse Harem, Monster Romance, Mythical Creatures, Portal, Psychic Powers, Revenge, Science-Fiction Romance, Seasonal, Secret Royalty, Shape Shifters, Steampunk, Superpowers, Time Travel, Urban Fantasy, Vampires, Werewolves, Witches/Wizards, Zodiac.

NOTES:

KNIGHT OR SQUIRE?

The Meet Cute setup: MC1 is an A+ student, and after years of study, their dream to conjure up or track down a fabled Magical Item (the equivalent of Excalibur, Thor's Hammer, Holy Grail, etc) is about to come true when suddenly classmate and general delinquent MC2 accidentally acquires the Magical Item with no effort?

Will uptight MC1 kneel and pledge allegiance to slacker MC2 or refuse to be subservient? And when they're forced to look at MC2 from a new perspective, will MC1 be able to resist falling in love with this diamond in the rough?

Suggested Paranormal Genre/Subgenre: Academy.

Suggested Classic Romance Trope(s): Opposites Attract.

Complimentary Romance Tropes and Paranormal Subgenres: Action and Adventure, Christmas, Curses, Dark Romance, Deities, Demons and Devils, Destiny, Divine Intervention, Dragons, Fae, Fairytale Retelling, Fated Mates, Found Family, Historical, Immortals, LitRPG, Medieval, Monster Romance, Mythical Creatures, Psychic Powers, Reverse Harem, Secret Royalty, Shape Shifters, Soul Mates, Steampunk, Superpowers, Time Travel, Urban Fantasy, Vampires, Werewolves, Witches/Wizards, Zodiac.

NOTES:

LAB PARTNERS

The Meet Cute setup: When MC1 meets MC2 on the first day of school, they're instant enemies. Did MC2 accidentally set MC1's books on fire? Maybe MC1 made a cross cultural faux pas and insulted MC2!

Whatever it was, they will have to get over it fast because guess who has just been paired up in class? To make matters worse, the results of their work will determine if they'll both get to continue at the Academy or will be sent home to a boring mortal life without magic!

Mix it up: Rather than becoming enemies, they're instant friends, but there's only one student spot open, and the classwork will determine who gets it! Will MC1 sacrifice their magic for their special someone?

Suggested Paranormal Genre/Subgenre: Academy.

Suggested Classic Romance Trope(s): Enemies to Lovers, Friends to Lovers.

Complimentary Romance Tropes and Paranormal Subgenres: Action and Adventure, Christmas, Curses, Dark Romance, Deities, Demons and Devils, Destiny, Divine Intervention, Dragons, Fae, Fairytale Retelling, Fated Mates, Found Family, GameLit, Genie in a Bottle, Psychic Powers, Science-Fiction Romance, Seasonal, Secret Royalty, Shape Shifters, Soul Mates, Steampunk, Superpowers, Time Travel, Urban Fantasy, Vampires, Werewolves, Witches/Wizards, Zodiac.

NOTES:

LOSS OF CONTROL

The Meet Cute setup: While starting at a magic academy can be exciting for freshmen, it's clear from day one that the lessons aren't just there to fill in time! When MC1 tries to show off their powers to their brand new friends, they totally lose control in front of MC2!

Is MC2 injured, or are they an older student who knows how to fix the situation?

It's important to understand that the nature of the magical power and resulting accident should vary depending on the kind of reaction you want to elicit from the Reader. So for a humorous RomCom situation make sure no one is hurt or terribly injured, but for a darker tone of romance, such as a Bully Romance, then serious consequences could be appropriate.

Suggested Paranormal Genre/Subgenre: Academy.

Suggested Classic Romance Trope(s): RomCom

Complimentary Romance Tropes and Paranormal Subgenres: Bully Romance, Curses, Dark Romance, Deities, Demons and Devils, Destiny, Divine Intervention, Dragons, Fae, Fairytale Retelling, Fated Mates, Found Family, GameLit, Genie in a Bottle, Ghosts, Harem/Reverse Harem, Historical, Immortals, LitRPG, Mythical Creatures, Portal, Psychic Powers, Reverse Harem, Science-Fiction Romance, Seasonal, Secret Royalty, Shape Shifters, Soul Mates, Steampunk, Superpowers, Time Travel, Urban Fantasy, Vampires, Werewolves, Witches/Wizards, Zodiac.

NOTES:

LOVE POTION ACCIDENT

The Meet Cute setup: Victims of a mean-spirited prank, such as a fake Valentine's Day date or gift, MC1 and MC2, fall head over heels for each other only to be humiliated when the rest of the class bursts out in laughter at their misfortune.

But even once the effects have worn off, MC2 can no longer look past the wallflower, and MC1 can't forget the soft center they once saw in rebellious MC2…

Can they find love again now they know what to look for?

Considerations: Don't forget, someone set this prank up. Who? And what were their motivations? Or maybe it didn't go to plan. What if this third party had intended the potion for themselves and one of the MCs? But which one?

Suggested Paranormal Genre/Subgenre: Academy.

Suggested Classic Romance Trope(s): Fake Dating, Opposites Attract.

Complimentary Romance Tropes and Paranormal Subgenres: Blind Date, Bully Romance, Curses, Deities, Demons and Devils, Destiny, Divine Intervention, Dragons, Fae, Fairytale Retelling, Fated Mates, Found Family, GameLit, Genie in a Bottle, Ghosts, Historical, Psychic Powers, Revenge, Seasonal, Secret Royalty, Shape Shifters, Steampunk, Superpowers, Valentine's Day, Vampires, Werewolves, Witches/Wizards, Zodiac.

NOTES:

ROOMMATES AT WAR

The Meet Cute setup: MC1 arrives at the Academy excited to start a new chapter in their lives! The only problem? Their territorial roommate MC2 raises force field barriers around every item they don't want to be touched.

MC1 can only deal with so many electric shocks before they snap and retaliate or transfer to a new dorm. But what if MC2's possessive nature extends to when another suitor comes sniffing around MC1 for a date to the school dance?

Can MC1 put their past clashes aside long enough to admit they have secretly liked oddball MC2 all along? And what will happen when MC2's walls finally come down?

Suggested Paranormal Genre/Subgenre: Academy.

Suggested Classic Romance Trope(s): Enemies to Lovers, Forced Proximity.

Complimentary Romance Tropes and Paranormal Subgenres: Bully Romance, Curses, Cyborgs, Dark Romance, Found Family, GameLit, Genie in a Bottle, Ghosts, LitRPG, Monster Romance, Mythical Creatures, Psychic Powers, Science-Fiction Romance, Seasonal, Superpowers, Witches/Wizards, Zodiac.

NOTES:

THEME OR SUBGENRE

~ ALIENS ~

BARTERED BRIDE

The Meet Cute setup: Alien MC2 has fallen in instalove with human MC1, and sets out to get their intended mate at any cost.

When human MC1 discovers their father has set up an arranged marriage in exchange for treasure and wealth, there's only one thing for sure–MC1 is glad to see the back of their wastrel dad and initially plans to use the wedding day to escape their oppressed and dull existence.

But what surprises MC1 is the fortune alien MC2 was willing to pay for their hand in marriage. Should they stick to the plan and run away or take a chance on this alien encounter?

With MC2 determined to make MC1 happy, maybe their future could be brighter than anticipated?

Suggested Paranormal Genre/Subgenre: Aliens.

Suggested Classic Romance Trope(s): Instalove, Royalty.

Complimentary Romance Tropes and Paranormal Subgenres: Action and Adventure, Arranged Marriage, Blind Date, Bounty Hunter, Bully Romance, Cyborgs, Fated Mates, GameLit, Genie in a Bottle, Kidnapping, LitRPG, Monster Romance, Psychic Powers, Science-Fiction Romance, Secret Royalty, Shape Shifters, Soul Mates.

NOTES:

DIPLOMAT TO THE ALIEN KING

The Meet Cute setup: First contact has been made, and Earth is in crisis as a looming alien race threatens to enslave all mankind. Human MC1 is sent on a diplomatic mission to Alien King MC2 as an ambassador for humankind.

From MC2's heated gazes, probing questions and surprisingly gentle touches at their first meeting, will MC1 be able to teach MC2 to value and respect humans rather than enslaving them?

Considerations: If MC1 is a last-minute replacement and out of their depth, or a well-trained soldier with a secret agenda to assassinate MC2, this character foundation will dramatically change the core story, from slow-burn romance to action-packed. So think first about what tone you want to convey when choosing personality attributes or backstories.

Suggested Paranormal Genre/Subgenre: Aliens.

Suggested Classic Romance Trope(s): Age Gap, Royalty.

Complimentary Romance Tropes and Paranormal Subgenres: Action and Adventure, Arranged Marriage, Kidnapping, Science-Fiction Romance, Secret Baby, Secret Royalty.

NOTES:

THEME OR SUBGENRE ~ ALIENS ~

KIDNAPPED BRIDE & THE DEVOTED WARRIOR

The Meet Cute setup: Human MC1's world is being invaded by powerful aliens! During the invasion, MC1 is kidnapped by alien warrior MC2 but once imprisoned on their craft they discover MC2 has more relatable qualities than expected–and in many ways is Better Than Human, compared to their previous romantic prospects.

Considerations: Think about MC2's motives for choosing MC1 out of the population. Was it love/lust at first sight? Was MC2 secretly in a panic and so desperate to get back to the mothership they just grabbed the first human they saw?

And after the initial abduction, what reasons could they have to keep this human specimen around? Is MC1 feisty and MC2 timid or vice versa?

Suggested Paranormal Genre/Subgenre: Aliens.

Suggested Classic Romance Trope(s): Bodyguard/Military, Opposites Attract.

Complimentary Romance Tropes and Paranormal Subgenres: Action and Adventure, Divine Intervention, Found Family, Kidnapping, Science-Fiction Romance.

NOTES:

MAIL ORDER BRIDE & THE ALIEN RANCHER

The Meet Cute setup: On a primitive terraformed planet, Alien Rancher MC1 is in need of a bride. Who will fit the bill? Is MC2 painstakingly picked out of a catalog or randomly selected by slavers? And once they have MC2 safe and sound on their own home planet, how far will they go to win their affection?

While this wild and rustic life isn't the exotic off-world destination MC2 had envisioned when they were sent to this planet, with a devoted and attractive alien MC1 at their beck and call, they might be swayed to go along for the ride!

A futuristic twist on a popular historic old-west trope: *Mail-order bride.*

Suggested Paranormal Genre/Subgenre: Aliens.

Suggested Classic Romance Trope(s): Fish-out-of-water, Instalove.

Complimentary Romance Tropes and Paranormal Subgenres: Arranged Marriage, Cyborgs, Destiny, Divine Intervention, Found Family, Single Parent, Small Town, Science-Fiction Romance.

NOTES:

PRIZE FOR THE ALIEN GLADIATOR

The Meet Cute setup: Alien MC1 has fought long and hard in the dangerous gladiator battles on their home planet, and with their final victory they are given the prize of a gorgeous human MC2.

Fully intending to retire and enjoy retirement, MC1 shows MC2 which other areas they possess physical prowess... Nothing could force MC1 to return to their previous line of work, except perhaps if the apple of their eye, MC2, is kidnapped to be sold on the black market.

Suggested Paranormal Genre/Subgenre: Aliens.

Suggested Classic Romance Trope(s): Alpha, Bodyguard/Military, Instalove.

Complimentary Romance Tropes and Paranormal Subgenres: Action and Adventure, Dark Romance, Kidnapping, Science-Fiction Romance. Workplace.

NOTES:

SANCTUARY WITH THE ALIEN MONKS

The Meet Cute setup: Earth is destroyed, and human MC1 has escaped the slavers who have done the horrible deed and approaches an alien monastery that promises neutral ground and safety from intergalactic marauders while gathering their strength and plotting their revenge.

MC2, as a protector and peacemaker, does everything within their power to make MC1 feel welcome and happy as is commanded by their religious and moral code–and much to MC1's relief, they realize celibacy isn't a value they adhere to.

Can MC1's new desire for sexy alien MC2 sate their desire for revenge?

Suggested Paranormal Genre/Subgenre: Aliens.

Suggested Classic Romance Trope(s): Bodyguard/Military.

Complimentary Romance Tropes and Paranormal Subgenres: Action and Adventure, Found Family, Portal, Reverse Harem.

NOTES:

THEME OR SUBGENRE ~ ALIENS ~

SEAHORSE ALIEN DADDY

The Meet Cute setup: Whether human female MC1 was captured, traded, arranged or married to Seahorse Alien MC2 the result is equally magnificent. Where in her primitive hometown planet she would have been the one bearing the domestic load according to her planet's transitional values, her new spouse has subverted all her expectations - in their relationship she won't even have to deal with childbirth! At their wedding and first meeting, MC2 is a little confused by his new bride fist pumping in triumph, but if it's a human custom MC1 values perhaps he will try joining in.

Suggested Paranormal Genre/Subgenre: Aliens.

Suggested Classic Romance Trope(s): Fish-out-of-water, Instalove, Marriage of Convenience.

Complimentary Romance Tropes and Paranormal Subgenres: Found Family, Science-Fiction Romance, Small Town, Soul Mates.

NOTES:

TERRAFORMING TINDER

The Meet Cute setup: When settling on a new planet to terraform in a universe with many planets and species, there is no guarantee of finding a human mate. Enter the dating agency "We're All Aliens Here," ready to solve everybody's compatibility quandaries. Swipe No on the Slimes and swipe Yes on Sexy Humanoid Aliens.

When MC1 is matched with their ideal fantasy candidate, MC2, they can't believe their luck–maybe destiny works better when you're up among the stars.

Suggested Paranormal Genre/Subgenre: Aliens.

Suggested Classic Romance Trope(s): Instalove, RomCom.

Complimentary Romance Tropes and Paranormal Subgenres: Blind Date, Destiny, Fated Mates, Science-Fiction Romance, Soul Mates, Valentine's Day.

NOTES:

WAR TROPHY WIFE

The Meet Cute setup: Alien veteran MC1 is in want of a wife. And for their incredible feats of bravery they are awarded a human of their own– a prized possession due to their rarity and universally acknowledged beauty!

When MC1 meets MC2, sparks fly as MC1 falls in Instalove, but MC2 must prove they are more than just a trophy. With a loyal and proven warrior like MC1 onside, perhaps MC2 will not only get their own happily ever after but will begin the revival of the Human Age.

Suggested Paranormal Genre/Subgenre: Aliens.

Suggested Classic Romance Trope(s): Instalove, Bodyguard/Military.

Complimentary Romance Tropes and Paranormal Subgenres: Action and Adventure, Blind Date, Bounty Hunter, Kidnapping, Portal, Science-Fiction Romance, Secret Royalty, Single Parent.

NOTES:

~ ANGELS ~

ANGEL TRAINING DROPOUT

The Meet Cute setup: In order to uphold the impeccable standards required of angels, a strict training regimen is adhered to for the greater good of the cosmic order.

On guardian angel MC1's first mission to the human world, human MC2 steps in before MC1 can intercede.

MC2 risks their life to save a child from a deadly accident.

As MC1 falls for human MC2 against every protocol, they begin to ask can something that feels so good really be that bad?

Suggested Paranormal Genre/Subgenre: Angels.

Suggested Classic Romance Trope(s): Fish-out-of-water, Friends to Lovers.

Complimentary Romance Tropes and Paranormal Subgenres: Demons and Devils, Destiny, Divine Intervention, Christmas, Single Parent, Small Town, Soul Mates.

NOTES:

AVENGING ANGEL

The Meet Cute setup: Angel MC1 has tunnel vision for vengeance for their lost love, and they have been chasing down the demons responsible for over a thousand years. What will become of them when the last Demon is slain?

When they cross paths with MC2, their jaw drops as their heart skips a beat.

They never thought they would feel anything like this again–but is it worth the risk to MC2 when there are demons out there? What will chasing MC2 cost them? And would it be worth the reward?

Considerations: What if MC2 is related to one of the demons responsible? Would MC1 be able to halt their path of vengeance and learn to process their grief without bloodshed for the sake of a happy future?

Internal conflicts like this can make those decisions harder for your characters and that much more satisfying for your happy ending.

Suggested Paranormal Genre/Subgenre: Angels.

Suggested Classic Romance Trope(s): Opposites Attract.

Complimentary Romance Tropes and Paranormal Subgenres: Divine Intervention, Revenge.

NOTES:

CAUGHT OUT BY A CLEAN WINDOW

The Meet Cute setup: Birds aren't the only winged creatures to find clean windows hard to see, and when Angel MC1 splats into MC2's office window, they'll do everything they can to revive them.

When MC1 comes to and sees MC2's beautiful features, there's one question on their mind: Is MC2 an angel, or did they seriously mess up?

Suggested Paranormal Genre/Subgenre: Angels.

Suggested Classic Romance Trope(s): Alpha, Forced Proximity, Instalove, RomCom.

Complimentary Romance Tropes and Paranormal Subgenres: Christmas, Curses, Demons and Devils, Destiny, Divine Intervention, Fairytale Retelling, Fated Mates, Found Family, Medical Romance, Mythical Creatures, Seasonal, Small Town, Soul Mates, Valentine's Day.

NOTES:

THEME OR SUBGENRE ~ ANGELS ~

DARK ANGELS

The Meet Cute setup: Not all Angels are goody-two-shoes, and when on-the-run MC1 crosses paths with stormy Angel MC2, they know they are in trouble... But with pecs like that and a flaming sword that can cut a demon clean in two, maybe MC2 could provide them with the protection MC1 desperately needs-if they can pay the price.

Luckily, MC2 doesn't trade in USD. They would rather taste the forbidden fruit, and MC1 looks exactly the part.

Suggested Paranormal Genre/Subgenre: Angels.

Suggested Classic Romance Trope(s): Bodyguard/Military, Instalove, Opposites Attract, Romantic Suspense.

Complimentary Romance Tropes and Paranormal Subgenres: Bounty Hunter, Bully Romance, Curses, Dark Romance, Demons and Devils, Destiny, Divine Intervention, Dragons, Fae, Fairytale Retelling, Fated Mates, Immortals, Mafia, Monster Romance, Mythical Creatures, Portal, Revenge, Urban Fantasy.

NOTES:

GUARDIAN ANGEL BLUNDER

The Meet Cute setup: Guardian Angels are always there, hidden helpers secretly sorting out all the snags to keep you safe... which is why when GA MC1 trips on their wings and takes a tumble, they're horrified that they've not only been seen but they require the help of human MC2 to get them back on their feet.

Is this the start of a beautiful romance, or are there reasons why the two races are forbidden to mix?

It's time MC2 teaches MC1 the meaning of a human saying: Nothing worth having ever comes easy.

Suggested Paranormal Genre/Subgenre: Angels.

Suggested Classic Romance Trope(s): RomCom.

Complimentary Romance Tropes and Paranormal Subgenres: Academy, Christmas, Destiny, Divine Intervention, Fairytale Retelling, Historical, Immortals, Seasonal, Secret Royalty, Valentine's Day.

NOTES:

PENTHOUSE HIRED HELP

The Meet Cute setup: When MC1 took on a job as a cleaner in the tallest building in the city, they had no idea just how far their world was about to be opened up.

While cleaning the luxurious top-floor apartment well above the clouds, MC1 misses the memo instructing the windows must be kept open at all times. And fearful of heights, MC1 slams them shut to stifle their sense of vertigo. After all, who in their right mind would want a window that opens this high in the sky?

A creature with wings, of course! How will Angel MC2 react when they have to knock on their own 'door' to be let in by MC1?

Suggested Paranormal Genre/Subgenre: Angels.

Suggested Classic Romance Trope(s): Cinderella.

Complimentary Romance Tropes and Paranormal Subgenres: Christmas, Curses, Destiny, Divine Intervention, Fairytale Retelling, Immortals, Mythical Creatures, Seasonal, Valentine's Day.

NOTES:

WARRIOR ANGEL

The Meet Cute setup: Archangel MC1 takes their job seriously, whether it's fighting in wars of a cosmological scale or guarding the gates of heaven.

Today, however, they were supposed to be standing guard over MC2. Unfortunately, MC2 doesn't like being watched. After a failed escape attempt, and a rough and tumble tussle where MC1 accidentally left a few bruises and MC2 ended up with a fistful of freshly pulled feathers, they both agree to make a few compromises. Maybe they'll find they work better together than they thought.

Suggested Paranormal Genre/Subgenre: Angels.

Suggested Classic Romance Trope(s): Bodyguard/Military, Enemies to Lovers, Grumpy Sunshine.

Complimentary Romance Tropes and Paranormal Subgenres: Bounty Hunter, Demons and Devils, Destiny, Divine Intervention, Fairytale Retelling, Fated Mates, Found Family, Historical, Mythical Creatures..

NOTES:

THEME OR SUBGENRE

~ ANOMALIES AND ACCIDENTS ~

BODY SWAP

The Meet Cute setup: oworkers MC1 and MC2 tangle with an object that switches their bodies! How will they take this personal intrusion into each other's lives?

Will mudance office banter transition into deeper conversations as they learn to respect and care for one another on a more intimate level? If they start out as enemies, can they put their differences aside to work together to uncover the secret of the object so they can switch back to their original bodies?

Considerations: Is the object magical, future or alien-tech, or even divine in nature?

Suggested Paranormal Genre/Subgenre: Urban Fantasy, Science-Fiction Romance.

Suggested Classic Romance Trope(s): Enemies to Lovers, Friends to Lovers, RomCom.

Complimentary Romance Tropes and Paranormal Subgenres: Action and Adventure, Curses, Destiny, Divine Intervention, GameLit, Genie in a Bottle, Seasonal, Steampunk, Superpowers, Time Travel, Witches/Wizards, Zodiac..

NOTES:

THEME OR SUBGENRE ~ ANOMALIES AND ACCIDENTS ~

BODY SWAP PET

The Meet Cute setup: Archeologist MC1 has just returned home from an adventure with a mysterious artifact that requires delicate handling.

Neighbour MC2 enters the apartment to inform them that their cat is fed and alive–although they never want to pet sit again because they HATE the furry little critter.

But as MC1 rummages to get some cash to hand over to MC2, MC2 touches the artifact and magically switches bodies with the cat they hate!

Now MC1 is responsible not only for their neighbor in their cat's body but their cat in MC2's body–which is currently destroying the apartment in a panic and trying to climb the curtains!

How will they care for them both? How will MC2 communicate, and how will they feel about seeing their own human body curled up on MC1's bed, begging for pats and ear scratches?

Suggested Paranormal Genre/Subgenre: Cozy Fantasy.

Suggested Classic Romance Trope(s): Forced Proximity, RomCom.

Complimentary Romance Tropes and Paranormal Subgenres: Action and Adventure, Christmas, Curses, Destiny, Seasonal, Single Parent, Small Town, Soul Mates.

NOTES:

THEME OR SUBGENRE ~ ANOMALIES AND ACCIDENTS ~

DOCTOR, DOCTOR

The Meet Cute setup: A clerical error sees small-town doctor MC1 receive the complete medical records of newcomer and loner MC2. Records that reveal medical experiments done on MC2 in their youth...

MC2 has never seen their own medical records, and despite blank periods in their memory, they have never had reason to seek out the cause. So how do they react when the nosey town doctor calls them in for a thorough discussion and examination?

Will MC1 be able to balance their empathy and curiosity, especially when MC2 may have dangerous hidden abilities? And how will MC2 feel about the first person in their life to care enough to ask if they're okay?

Suggested Paranormal Genre/Subgenre: Science-Fiction Romance.

Suggested Classic Romance Trope(s): Grumpy Sunshine.

Complimentary Romance Tropes and Paranormal Subgenres: Medical Romance, Psychic Powers, Revenge, Shape Shifters, Small Town, Werewolves, Witches/Wizards, Zodiac..

NOTES:

THEME OR SUBGENRE ~ ANOMALIES AND ACCIDENTS ~

IMMACULATE CONCEPTION

The Meet Cute setup: MC1 finds themselves suddenly and inexplicably pregnant and tests reveal it's MC2's child!

How will that first conversation go, and will they have been abducted by aliens, been victim to a drug that affects short-term memory, or been part of a larger military plot? Could MC2 have a long-lost identical twin?

Suggested Paranormal Genre/Subgenre: Science-Fiction Romance.

Suggested Classic Romance Trope(s): Fake Dating, Fish-out-of-water, Forced Proximity, Marriage of Convenience.

Complimentary Romance Tropes and Paranormal Subgenres: Action and Adventure, Aliens, Angels, Arranged Marriage, Blind Date, Destiny, Divine Intervention, Dragons, Fae, Kidnapping, LitRPG, Psychic Powers, Secret Baby, Urban Fantasy, Zodiac..

NOTES:

THEME OR SUBGENRE ~ ANOMALIES AND ACCIDENTS ~

INVISIBLE MC

The Meet Cute setup: While trying to earn some money participating in experimental testing trials, unlucky MC1 turns invisible at random times with no explanation and needs scientist MC2's assistance to survive–and to figure out how to reverse it!

How will MC2 have to protect MC1? Do they escape the tests and go on the run? Could the military or shady corporations be after them? What kinds of information will MC1 be able to overhear when unseen, and can MC2 fall for someone they are unable to see?

Considerations: Think about how this troubling condition will affect MC1's family and daily life. Whether the problems are small and domestic or have large worldwide ramifications should impact the overall tone and theme of the story–from a family-friendly RomCom to an action-packed political thriller.

Suggested Paranormal Genre/Subgenre: Paranormal Thriller.

Suggested Classic Romance Trope(s): Fish-out-of-water, Grumpy Sunshine, Romantic Suspense.

Complimentary Romance Tropes and Paranormal Subgenres: Action and Adventure, Aliens, Bounty Hunter, Found Family, GameLit, LitRPG, Psychic Powers, Regency, Steampunk, Superpowers, Time Travel, Urban Fantasy.

NOTES:

THEME OR SUBGENRE ~ ANOMALIES AND ACCIDENTS ~
MEMORY ISSUES

The Meet Cute setup: MC1 lands in an unfamiliar town with no idea who they are or why they're there. Luckily childhood sweetheart MC2 recognises them and takes them in until they can figure out what's going on.

What if MC1 has escaped after having had their memory wiped and there's now a dangerous third-party threat after them? And will the heart remember what the brain has forgotten and deliver these two a second chance at love?

Suggested Paranormal Genre/Subgenre: Urban Fantasy, New Adult.

Suggested Classic Romance Trope(s): Second Chance Romance, Romantic Suspense.

Complimentary Romance Tropes and Paranormal Subgenres: Action and Adventure, Aliens, Bounty Hunter, Science-fiction Romance.

NOTES:

THEME OR SUBGENRE ~ ANOMALIES AND ACCIDENTS ~

MYSTERY DISAPPEARANCES

The Meet Cute setup: MC1 and MC2 have never met before, but when a mutual friend disappears without a trace their paths are irreversibly intertwined.

How will each of them contribute to solving the case, and what differences in motive will provide a conflict that will delay their happy ending? Can they trust each other?

Perhaps MC1 has a different motivation than MC2. For example, one MC wants to keep the disappearance a secret for legal or political reasons, or the missing person has disappeared with something they are desperate to get back.

Suggested Paranormal Genre/Subgenre: Fantasy Mystery, Young Adult.

Suggested Classic Romance Trope(s): Romantic Suspense.

Complimentary Romance Tropes and Paranormal Subgenres: Action and Adventure, Aliens, Bounty Hunter, GameLit, Kidnapping, Vampires.

NOTES:

THEME OR SUBGENRE ~ ANOMALIES AND ACCIDENTS ~ PORTALS

The Meet Cute setup: MC1 falls through a portal only to be discovered by MC2. They will need MC2's assistance to survive in this world and find a way home, but perhaps MC1 has exactly what this new world needs to have its own happy ending.

Portals are equally great for Time-Travel Romances with real-world historical settings, or entirely made-up and Fantastical settings.

While part of the conflict will be influenced by one or both of the couple knowing that there's another life that has been left behind, don't forget to instill core character conflicts, such as classic opposites attract or Grumpy Sunshine personalities. "Cultural" loggerheads and mis-understandings can lead to some engaging situations.

Suggested Paranormal Genre/Subgenre: Portals, Young Adult, Dystopian.

Suggested Classic Romance Trope(s): Fish-out-of-water, Grumpy Sunshine, Opposites Attract.

Complimentary Romance Tropes and Paranormal Subgenres: Academy, Action and Adventure, Arranged Marriage, Destiny, Divine Intervention, Fae, Fairytale Retelling, Found Family, GameLit, Science-fiction Romance, Time Travel.

NOTES:

THEME OR SUBGENRE ~ ANOMALIES AND ACCIDENTS ~

SECRET WORLD BENEATH THE ICE

The Meet Cute setup: No-nonsense Researcher MC1 and Carefree Guide MC2 find themselves stranded in Antarctica after a storm turns their vessel back. They have enough supplies to sustain them until the next rescue attempt, but they make a discovery that puts all thoughts of home to the back of their minds!

The melting ice caps have revealed a secret–wonderful or terrible. Is it a clue to a lost civilization? Alien tech?

How does each MC view the discovery? Do they want to share it with the world or keep it to themselves? Is it simply a way to make a fast buck? Does someone else know what is hidden here and, will they come looking?

And will the adrenaline of a near-death experience be enough to make MC1 and MC2 admit to the secret feelings they've been hiding beneath their own icy exteriors?

Suggested Paranormal Genre/Subgenre: Science-Fiction Romance, Paranormal Thriller.

Suggested Classic Romance Trope(s): Age Gap, Forced Proximity, Opposites Attract.

Complimentary Romance Tropes and Paranormal Subgenres: Action and Adventure, Aliens, Found Family, GameLit, Mythical Creatures, Portal, Psychic Powers, Steampunk, Superpowers, Time Travel.

NOTES:

THEME OR SUBGENRE ~ ANOMALIES AND ACCIDENTS ~

TRAPPED IN A SMART HOUSE

The Meet Cute setup: echnology is great until it stops working. Homeowner MC1 and Repair Person MC2 become trapped in a Smart House powered by artificial intelligence when a faulty sensor thinks there's a threat outside and the inhabitants need to be locked in the panic room.

What if MC1 is hiding a shapeshifter secret and the moon is about to rise? Or what if one is a Vampire who is getting mighty hungry?

What other secret could Homeowner MC1 desperately not want stranger MC2 to uncover about them? Maybe they're not originally from Earth? Or maybe the ghost of their exe just won't go away?

Suggested Paranormal Genre/Subgenre: Cozy Fantasy.

Suggested Classic Romance Trope(s): Forced Proximity, RomCom.

Complimentary Romance Tropes and Paranormal Subgenres: Aliens, Ghosts, Science-Fiction Romance, Shape Shifter, Werewolves, Vampires..

NOTES:

~ CURSES ~

CURSED JEWELS AND HEIRLOOMS

The Meet Cute setup: Clueless rich-kid MC1 inherits a cursed object when a distant relative dies. The item could be ancient Egyptian jewelry, looted pirate treasure, or a mysterious Incan box. Whatever the item is, it spells trouble!

Can MC1 ward off the bad luck long enough to find out who the original owner is and return the sacred object?

They'll need street-smart MC2's help to decode the mystery, but will MC2 be able to put their love of MC1 above their desire to keep the valuable treasure for themselves? Maybe MC2 was planning on stealing it all along?

Mix it Up: Combine a Cursed Object with a Portal story and what if this troublesome heirloom transports our luckless MC back in time to when the gem was first stolen or cursed?

Suggested Paranormal Genre/Subgenre: Young Adult.

Suggested Classic Romance Trope(s): Opposites Attract.

Complimentary Romance Tropes and Paranormal Subgenres: Action and Adventure, Curses, Portal, Time Travel.

NOTES:

LYING MIRROR

The Meet Cute setup: Stuck in a rut, Sunshine MC1 believes in destiny, and when they find a Magic Mirror that heralds Grumpy Loner MC2 as their protector for a noble quest which promises adventure and fortune, it's a dream come true. But what if the mirror only lies?

When MC1 hunts down the Not-Chosen-One MC2 for the quest, how far along the journey will they get before they find they've taken the wrong path?

And can two people not destined for each other make it work even if it's against what is written in the stars?

Suggested Paranormal Genre/Subgenre: Fairytale Retelling,

Suggested Classic Romance Trope(s): Bodyguard/Military, Enemies to Lovers, Grumpy Sunshine, Opposites Attract.

Complimentary Romance Tropes and Paranormal Subgenres: Action and Adventure, Curses, Beauty and the Beast Retelling, LitRPG, Urban Fantasy.

NOTES:

THEME OR SUBGENRE ~ CURSES ~

PANDORA'S BOX

The Meet Cute setup: Antiques should come with warning labels, or at least that is what MC1 believes after accidentally opening a box and unleashing chaos on the world.

Just like in the myth of old, can newly-freed Genji/curse-victim MC2 persuade MC1 not everything that comes out of the box is bad when there's hope for love to grow?

Suggested Paranormal Genre/Subgenre: Fairytale Retelling, Mythical Creatures.

Suggested Classic Romance Trope(s): Age Gap, Enemies to Lovers, Forced Proximity, Friends to Lovers.

Complimentary Romance Tropes and Paranormal Subgenres: Academy, Action and Adventure, Christmas, Curses, Destiny, GameLit, Genie in a Bottle, Historical, Immortals, Urban Fantasy, Vacation.

NOTES:

SLEEPING BEAUTY TWIST

The Meet Cute setup: MC1 fell victim to a sleeping curse that could only be reversed by True Love's Kiss.

Luckily their fairy godmother managed to subvert the curse into a slow-acting reduced version which would gradually extend their nights until they fall into a coma–but during their sleeping hours, they can traverse into their True Love's dreams and try to communicate to them how to find them and what to do.

But what if when they find them, MC2 is dreaming of another? Will they ever be able to fall for the person who crashed into their dreams and punched them in the face?

Suggested Paranormal Genre/Subgenre: Fairytale Retelling.

Suggested Classic Romance Trope(s): Enemies to Lovers, Royalty.

Complimentary Romance Tropes and Paranormal Subgenres: Academy, Christmas, Curses, Destiny, Divine Intervention, Dragons, Fae, Found Family, GameLit, Genie in a Bottle, Science-Fiction Romance, Seasonal, Secret Royalty, Urban Fantasy, Witches/Wizards.

NOTES:

UNLUCKY IN LOVE

The Meet Cute setup: Disaster magnet and risk taker Extrovert MC1 has broken so many mirrors and walked under so many ladders their bad luck is guaranteed to last more than a lifetime.

But when they fall in Instalove with Uptight Introvert MC2 while pitching a business deal or cunning heist, they'll do just about anything to turn their luck around and win them. Through accidents and mayhem they'll soon discover love has nothing to do with luck.

Suggested Paranormal Genre/Subgenre: Paranormal Romance, Heists.

Suggested Classic Romance Trope(s): Instalove, Grumpy Sunshine, Opposites Attract, RomCom.

Complimentary Romance Tropes and Paranormal Subgenres: Action and Adventure, Bounty Hunter, Curses, Divine Intervention, Found Family, GameLit, Mafia, Science-Fiction Romance, Seasonal, Steampunk, Superpowers, Urban Fantasy..

NOTES:

~ DEITIES ~

DEITY IN HUMAN SKIN

The Meet Cute setup: Arrogant Deity MC1 hates being reminded that they are technically a 'lesser deity'. When one of the elder gods curses them into a human form to teach them humility, MC1 is forced to rely on a weak human, MC2, to help them adjust and find a way to restore their godly power.

Can they ever see MC2 as more than a humble human, and what will happen when MC2 threatens not to help them?

Their first exchange will set the tone for the rest of their relationship progression.

Suggested Paranormal Genre/Subgenre: Mythical Creatures, Paranormal Romance.

Suggested Classic Romance Trope(s): Alpha, RomCom.

Complimentary Romance Tropes and Paranormal Subgenres: Christmas, Curses, Divine Intervention, Fairytale Retelling, Immortals..

NOTES:

HALF-BLOOD DEITY

The Meet Cute setup: Half-Blood MC1 isn't quite godly enough for the gods or human enough for the humans. When invited to a party of other gods and half-gods, they meet MC2, sparking a rivalry that will see them find their place and their powers.

Little do they know this challenging first meeting will set them on a path where they'll discover they will fulfill their desires better together than apart.

Further Considerations: If you have two half-god MCs, which god were their parents, and under which circumstances were they raised? Is MC2 more familiar with the world of the gods? What reasons can you find for them to fight, and what shared experiences or values will allow them to connect?

Suggested Paranormal Genre/Subgenre: Mythical Creatures, Paranormal Romance.

Suggested Classic Romance Trope(s): Enemies to Lovers.

Complimentary Romance Tropes and Paranormal Subgenres: Academy, Action and Adventure, Arranged Marriage, Blind Date, Bully Romance, Curses, Dark Romance, Deities, Demons and Devils, Destiny, Divine Intervention, Monster Romance, Secret Royalty, Soul Mates, Zodiac.

NOTES:

HUNKY HEAVEN

The Meet Cute setup: When MC1 died and went to heaven, they didn't expect the afterlife to look like this. With a complex social system where everyone seems to be a more attractive version of their best selves, MC1 can't help but wonder why they still have scars and sets off on a journey to find answers.

Will deity MC2 be the one to convince them of the beauty they see lying inside?

Suggested Paranormal Genre/Subgenre: Mythical Creatures, Paranormal Romance, Fairytale Retelling.

Suggested Classic Romance Trope(s): Cinderella, Forced Proximity, Friends to Lovers.

Complimentary Romance Tropes and Paranormal Subgenres: Angels, Blind Date, Bully Romance, Dark Romance, Deities, Demons and Devils, Destiny, Divine Intervention, Fairytale Retelling, Fated Mates, Found Family, Immortals.

NOTES:

LESSER KNOWN DEITY

The Meet Cute setup: They say that the gods get their power from the number of worshippers and the quality of sacrifices... So when Wiccan MC1 starts up an "Adopt a Deity" program, setting up altars and supporters to resurrect the old and forgotten gods, they might come to realize some of them were forgotten for a reason.

Deity MC2 however, will see their heart for what it is worth and protect them from the wrath of their more vengeful contemporaries.

Perhaps by the end of their adventures, MC2 will be able to transition to a human form, and they can live out the rest of their days together.

Suggested Paranormal Genre/Subgenre: Mythical Creatures, Witches and Wizards.

Suggested Classic Romance Trope(s): Age Gap, Alpha, RomCom.

Complimentary Romance Tropes and Paranormal Subgenres: Academy, Angels, Arranged Marriage, Blind Date, Christmas, Dark Romance, Deities, Destiny, Divine Intervention, Fairytale Retelling, Immortals, Seasonal, Secret Royalty, Urban Fantasy, Valentine's Day, Witches/Wizards, Zodiac.

NOTES:

THEME OR SUBGENRE ~ DEITIES ~

LONELY HEARTS CLUB

The Meet Cute setup: MC1 Cupid is used to being overlooked and only asked for the service of their arrows, so when MC2 summons MC1 to instead attend as a Guest of Honor speaker to the Lonely Hearts Club they've founded for singletons, MC1 is both surprised and flattered.

Being valued and appreciated for their advice for the first time in centuries, Cupid falls head over heels for MC2.

Can Cupid's Instalove last when they find out MC2's true identity?

Suggested Paranormal Genre/Subgenre: Mythical Creatures, Paranormal Romance.

Suggested Classic Romance Trope(s): Fish-out-of-water, Instalove, Opposites Attract.

Complimentary Romance Tropes and Paranormal Subgenres: Angels, Divine Intervention, Fairytale Retelling, Fated Mates, Found Family, Historical, Immortals, Portal, Urban Fantasy, Witches/Wizards, Zodiac.

NOTES:

POSEIDON

The Meet Cute setup: Marine biologist MC1 loves the ocean and all its creatures. Poseidon MC2 sees their efforts to clean up ocean plastic, restore fish populations and revive the coral reef and decides to give them a hand.

What happens when Poseidon falls for vivacious MC1, who is determined to change the shape of the world despite not having any paranormal powers?

Will MC1 be able to trigger ambition in MC2, who has fallen into apathy over the last few centuries? And when MC2 has a vengeful streak, what will that mean for humanity? Can their love dampen MC2's temper enough to give them a happy ending?

Suggested Paranormal Genre/Subgenre: Mermaids, Mythical Creatures.

Suggested Classic Romance Trope(s): Fake Dating, Friends to Lovers.

Complimentary Romance Tropes and Paranormal Subgenres: Action and Adventure, Destiny, Divine Intervention, Found Family, Genie in a Bottle, Immortals, Monster Romance, Mythical Creatures, Revenge, Science-Fiction Romance, Seasonal, Vacation.

NOTES:

~ DEMONS AND DEVILS ~

ACCIDENTALLY SUMMONED

The Meet Cute setup: Cursive handwriting can be hard to read, and when novice spellcaster MC1 performs a spell from an old book but mispronounces the words, they unleash Demon MC2 upon the world.

Demon MC2 is bound to obey mortal MC1 but quickly realizes MC1 is unaware of this spell rule and plots to escape the ties that bind them.

How will MC1 discover their power over MC2, especially when MC2 is unwilling to share information? And from this first high-emotion scene, how will they start on their path to getting to know each other, forming empathy and falling into a cross-species romantic entanglement?

Suggested Paranormal Genre/Subgenre: Demons and Devils.

Suggested Classic Romance Trope(s): Enemies to Lovers, Forced Proximity.

Complimentary Romance Tropes and Paranormal Subgenres: Arranged Marriage, Blind Date, Christmas, Deities, Demons and Devils, Destiny, Divine Intervention, Fairytale Retelling, Genie in a Bottle, Immortals, Kidnapping, LitRPG, Monster Romance, Mythical Creatures, Portal, Single Parent, Zodiac.

NOTES:

THEME OR SUBGENRE ~ DEMONS AND DEVILS ~

BADDER THAN BAD

The Meet Cute setup: Devil MC1 gets more than they bargained for when they tried to mess with Human MC2.

What MC2 lacks in paranormal powers, they more than make up for in street smarts, and they won't hesitate to lie, cheat and steal whatever they need to get one over on MC1.

What will they do when the cat and mouse game ends and they finally have MC1 at their mercy? Kill them? Or kiss them?

Suggested Paranormal Genre/Subgenre: Demons and Devils.

Suggested Classic Romance Trope(s): Enemies to Lovers, Romantic Suspense, RomCom.

Complimentary Romance Tropes and Paranormal Subgenres: Action and Adventure, Angels, Bounty Hunter, Bully Romance, Curses, Dark Romance, Deities, Demons and Devils, Destiny, Divine Intervention, Kidnapping, Mafia, Monster Romance, Mythical Creatures, Revenge, Soul Mates.

NOTES:

BETROTHED TO THE DEVIL

The Meet Cute setup: Uh oh, MC1's dad made a deal with the devil twenty years ago for the hand of their firstborn child, and now they're coming to collect!

Little does Devil MC2 know they're in for more than they expect because MC1 has been training for this moment their whole life...

But will MC1 go through with their plan to overthrow the underworld when they start falling for their demonic spouse? Maybe they'll find they rule better together.

Suggested Paranormal Genre/Subgenre: Demons and Devils.

Suggested Classic Romance Trope(s): Marriage of Convenience, Opposites Attract, Royalty.

Complimentary Romance Tropes and Paranormal Subgenres: Arranged Marriage, Enemies to Lovers, Forced Proximity, Found Family, GameLit, Genie in a Bottle, Monster Romance, Mythical Creatures, Revenge, Urban Fantasy.

NOTES:

THEME OR SUBGENRE ~ DEMONS AND DEVILS ~

DEVIL IN SHEEP'S CLOTHING

The Meet Cute setup: Demon-for-hire MC1 looks like any other human and goes undercover to steal information from human MC2's business, but things go wrong immediately.

MC1 is busted for faking information on their resume. None the wiser as to their true demonic identity, MC2 attempts to blackmail MC1 into providing info on who hired them for this act of corporate sabotage.

Will MC1 attempt to complete their mission or will their betrayal cause a fallout on a cosmological scale?

Considerations: From their first meeting, think about how MC1's demonic nature will be revealed and other what mischievous and deceptive activities they could be up to that would set the tone for the rest of their relationship?

When they fall for each other, what would the cost be to demon MC1 when they choose to put a human first?

Suggested Paranormal Genre/Subgenre: Demons and Devils.

Suggested Classic Romance Trope(s): Alpha, Billionaire, Opposites Attract, Romantic Suspense.

Complimentary Romance Tropes and Paranormal Subgenres: Action and Adventure, Bully Romance, Christmas, Curses, Dark Romance, Deities, Demons and Devils, Destiny, Divine Intervention, Dragons, Fae, Fairytale Retelling, Immortals, Kidnapping, LitRPG, Mafia, Monster Romance, Mythical Creatures.

NOTES:

OTHER SIDE OF THE FENCE

The Meet Cute setup: When the Fallen Angels followed Lucifer to the pits of hell and became demons, that was a choice of autonomy and freedom that set them apart from the other heavenly beings for eternity.

But when Demon MC1 sees Angel MC2, they know they've fallen to an even deeper level of hell. How can they go on without them?

Will either of them be willing to forsake their own kind to make a future together?

Suggested Paranormal Genre/Subgenre: Demons and Devils.

Suggested Classic Romance Trope(s): Instalove, Opposites Attract.

Complimentary Romance Tropes and Paranormal Subgenres: Angels, Arranged Marriage, Blind Date, Christmas, Dark Romance, Deities, Demons and Devils, Destiny, Divine Intervention, Fairytale Retelling, Immortals, Kidnapping, Monster Romance, Mythical Creatures, Secret Royalty.

NOTES:

THEME OR SUBGENRE ~ DEMONS AND DEVILS ~

THE DEVIL IS IN THE DETAILS

The Meet Cute setup: Savvy Lawyer MC1 thinks they know what they are doing when signing a fixed-term contract with devil MC2 in exchange for a career boost, but they are about to learn never to trust a demon.

Because Devil MC2 doesn't want MC1's soul, they want MC''s hand in marriage.

Suggested Paranormal Genre/Subgenre: Demons and Devils.

Suggested Classic Romance Trope(s): Alpha, Fake Dating, Marriage of Convenience, RomCom, Royalty.

Complimentary Romance Tropes and Paranormal Subgenres: Arranged Marriage, Blind Date, Bully Romance, Christmas, Curses, Dark Romance, Deities, Demons and Devils, Destiny, Divine Intervention, Fairytale Retelling, Fated Mates, Harem/Reverse Harem, Kidnapping, Monster Romance, Mythical Creatures, Portal, Revenge, Science-Fiction Romance, Seasonal, Urban Fantasy.

NOTES:

UNDERWORLD SPOUSE

The Meet Cute setup: King of the Underworld MC1 is searching for a spouse. None of the recommended immortal candidates can handle the smell of sulphur, the pervasive screaming (even with a few sound-proofed rooms) or MC1's fiery personality.

Will MC1 finally meet their match when they bump into mortal goth MC2?

Suggested Paranormal Genre/Subgenre: Demons and Devils.

Suggested Classic Romance Trope(s): Fake Dating, Marriage of Convenience, RomCom, Royalty.

Complimentary Romance Tropes and Paranormal Subgenres: Action and Adventure, Arranged Marriage, Blind Date, Christmas, Curses, Destiny, Divine Intervention, Fairytale Retelling, Found Family, GameLit, Immortals, Kidnapping, LitRPG, Monster Romance, Mythical Creatures, Portal, Science-Fiction Romance, Seasonal, Secret Royalty, Urban Fantasy.

NOTES:

THEME OR SUBGENRE ~ DEMONS AND DEVILS ~

UNWILLING SACRIFICE

The Meet Cute setup: For centuries mortal MC1's town has offered a human tribute to local Demon MC2, who keeps the citizens safe in exchange for a temporary spouse. And as the demon has never been fussy, the town has gotten into the habit of sacrificing its most troublesome citizens...

Only when reluctant troublemaker MC1 arrives at MC2's lair do they realize their future might not be as bleak as they feared. Can two pariahs find their way into the future together?

And if MC1 is willing to commit in a way no other tribute has before–by binding their essences together–could they be the only partner MC2 ever needs for the rest of their immortal lives?

Further considerations: Is your demon character one of a kind, or are there more of them and if so where in the hierarchy does MC2 fit? What kind of slavery is MC1 initially entering into–does MC2 actually expect an arranged marriage, or do they just need a servant to keep the lair clean?

Suggested Paranormal Genre/Subgenre: Demons and Devils.

Suggested Classic Romance Trope(s): Cinderella, Forced Proximity, Marriage of Convenience.

Complimentary Romance Tropes and Paranormal Subgenres: Action and Adventure, Arranged Marriage, Blind Date, Bully Romance, Christmas, Curses, Dark Romance, Deities, Demons and Devils, Destiny, Divine Intervention, Fairytale Retelling, Harem/Reverse Harem, Immortals, Kidnapping, LitRPG, Mafia, Monster Romance, Mythical Creatures, Portal, Psychic Powers, Science-Fiction Romance, Seasonal, Urban Fantasy..

NOTES:

THEME OR SUBGENRE ~ DEMONS AND DEVILS ~

WORKING FOR THE DEVIL

The Meet Cute setup: MC1 knows the reputation CEO MC2 has as a total demon to work for. When they land their lucrative internship working directly under MC2, they discover that behind the rumors lies a truth they never could imagine...

Further considerations: Is MC1 an obedient submissive character archetype ready to do anything they're asked? From watering fake plants to an increasingly diabolical level of tasks, some of which might challenge their ethical values and capacity?

How would a goody-two-shoes, ready-to-please character deal with instructions like getting rid of a body? And how would you foreshadow the devious, playful or threatening aura of MC2's character from their first meeting?

Or will your MC1 be a headstrong character, ready to subvert MC2's instructions with creative rule-bending that commands their attention and gets their blood pumping?

Suggested Paranormal Genre/Subgenre: Demons and Devils.

Suggested Classic Romance Trope(s): Alpha, Billionaire, Bully, Celebrity, Forced Proximity.

Complimentary Romance Tropes and Paranormal Subgenres: Action and Adventure, Bully Romance, Dark Romance, Destiny, Divine Intervention, Fairytale Retelling, Fated Mates, Found Family, Mafia, Monster Romance, Mythical Creatures, Urban Fantasy, Zodiac.

NOTES:

THEME OR SUBGENRE

~ DRAGONS ~

ALL THAT GLITTERS IS NOT GOLD

The Meet Cute setup: It is just a regular night like any other in the club dragon shifter MC1 owns until they spot MC2 clothed in gold from across the room, and their eyes light up. MC1 knows what they want and is used to getting it...

MC2 is horrified by MC1's forthright lusty approach and throws their drink in MC1's face, declaring they would never go out with them in a thousand years!

Could MC2 have read some horrible rumors about MC1 in the tabloids? Or MC1 dumped MC2's best friend a few years ago. Maybe MC2 belongs to a rival family and had no idea MC1 owned this particular club.

Whatever the reason, there should be enough heat behind their exchange to show MC2 wants nothing but MC1's head on a plate. But it is not in a dragon's nature to take no for an answer. While trying to prove themselves, will their insta-lust grow into a deeper kind of love?

Suggested Paranormal Genre/Subgenre: Dragons

Suggested Classic Romance Trope(s): Alpha, Billionaire, Bully, Celebrity, Enemies to lovers, Instalove, Opposites Attract.

Complimentary Romance Tropes and Paranormal Subgenres: Action and Adventure, Blind Date, Bully Romance, Christmas, Curses, Dark Romance, Fairytale Retelling, Fated Mates, Found Family, Immortals, Kidnapping, Mafia, Medical Romance, Mythical Creatures, Secret Royalty, Shape Shifters, Urban Fantasy.

NOTES:

BABY DRAGON DAYCARE

The Meet Cute setup: Parenting is hard on a regular Tuesday. Throw in a shifter baby/child who can't control their transformation and can breathe fire? You're sure to be in for a wild ride.

Single parent shifter MC1 is at their wits end trying to raise their adorable little bundle of fire and hold down their home business. All they need is a few hours a day to work in peace without their offspring burning all their stock!

Luckily MC2 works at a preschool set up for kids who need… uh… special care and attention. Can they handle the little spitfire?

When MC1 is that smoking hot, and MC2's kid is that cute—when they're behaving—it might just be worth breaking the rule: No dating clients.

Suggested Paranormal Genre/Subgenre: Dragons

Suggested Classic Romance Trope(s): Age Gap, Forced Proximity.

Complimentary Romance Tropes and Paranormal Subgenres: Christmas, Curses, Destiny, Divine Intervention, Fairytale Retelling, Fated Mates, Found Family, Mythical Creatures, Seasonal, Shape Shifters, Single Parent, Small Town, Soul Mates.

NOTES:

CAPTURED ROYAL

The Meet Cute setup: Royal MC1 is kidnapped by dragon shifter MC2 and is overwhelmed by their powerful and mean demeanor.

Terrified, angry and determined to hate, MC1 plans to show MC2 that they are not the only one with bite. But will prolonged exposure allow them to fall for each other?

Perhaps MC2's reasons behind the kidnapping can be understood, especially if MC1's family have committed worse atrocities unbeknownst to MC1.

The ultimate test of faith and sacrifice for a control-loving dragon will be when MC2 lets MC1 go... Will MC2 run home and marry another? Or will they return for a happily ever after with the dragon?

Suggested Paranormal Genre/Subgenre: Dragons

Suggested Classic Romance Trope(s): Alpha, Enemies to Lovers, Grumpy Sunshine, RomCom, Romantic Suspense, Royalty.

Complimentary Romance Tropes and Paranormal Subgenres: Action and Adventure, Arranged Marriage, Bully Romance, Christmas, Divine Intervention, Fairytale Retelling, Fated Mates, Found Family, Kidnapping, Mythical Creatures, Portal, Science-Fiction Romance, Seasonal, Secret Royalty, Shape Shifters, Urban Fantasy.

NOTES:

FALLING FOR THE THIEF

The Meet Cute setup: It's said that if you steal from a dragon, you will never leave its lair alive.

Unfortunately for thief MC1, they have no idea that their target, MC2, is a dragon. When they bump into MC2 on their way out of the building with loot in hand, MC2 demands more than their life.

Perhaps MC2 needs a fake date or an heir from someone that will absolutely enrage their dragon of a mother, and lowly thief MC1 fits the bill.

But if a proud dragon falls in love with a thief, then sparks are guaranteed to fly.

Suggested Paranormal Genre/Subgenre: Dragons

Suggested Classic Romance Trope(s): Alpha, Billionaire, Bully, Enemies to Lovers, Fake Dating, Fish-Out-of-Water, Instalove, Mafia, Opposites Attract, Romantic Suspense, Royalty.

Complimentary Romance Tropes and Paranormal Subgenres: Action and Adventure, Bounty Hunter, Dark Romance, Fairytale Retelling, Fated Mates, Immortals, Kidnapping, Monster Romance, Mythical Creatures, Revenge, Reverse Harem, Science-Fiction Romance, Seasonal, Secret Royalty, Shape Shifters, Urban Fantasy, Zodiac.

NOTES:

INTO THE DRAGON'S DEN

The Meet Cute setup: MC1 is attending a job interview at dragon shifter MC2's business. Despite having limited work experience in the field, MC1 catches MC2's eye immediately and they are hired on the spot.

MC2's dominating stature and sexy aura take MC1's breath away and leave them shaking like a leaf. Will their eagerness to please and dangerous sense of curiosity lead them to discover MC2's shifter secret?

And what will both MCs do when they realize they have bitten off more than they can chew?

Further considerations: If you change the location and MC2's business, how does this change things?

Suggested Paranormal Genre/Subgenre: Dragons

Suggested Classic Romance Trope(s): Alpha, Billionaire, Fish-Out-of-Water, Grumpy Sunshine, Instalove, Opposites Attract.

Complimentary Romance Tropes and Paranormal Subgenres: Action and Adventure, Bully Romance, Christmas, Curses, Dark Romance, Fairytale Retelling, Fated Mates, Immortals, Mafia, Monster Romance, Mythical Creatures, Shape Shifters, Urban Fantasy.

NOTES:

THEME OR SUBGENRE ~ DRAGONS ~

MC WITH THE DRAGON TATTOO

The Meet Cute setup: There's nothing as sexy as a great tattoo on a body in peak physical condition, but when MC1 sees sexy MC2 working out at the gym, they think no harm will come from taking a sneaky selfie to share with their friends on social media.

But MC2's tattoo isn't just a pretty design. It is a brand belonging to the dragon brotherhood, a clan of shifters with a powerful and shady network spread all across the city. When MC1 posts the image they snapped on social media with the cheeky caption "my hot gym date" they've not only blown MC2's cover, they've painted a target on their back.

If only they hadn't taken that photo. If only they had checked their privacy settings on their app... It is too late for regrets because this adventure promises to be capital H level Hot.

Mix it up: What if MC2 isn't a dragon but is a Vampire or Fae?

Suggested Paranormal Genre/Subgenre: Dragons

Suggested Classic Romance Trope(s): Celebrity, Fish-out-of-water, Forced Proximity, Grumpy Sunshine, Romantic Suspense.

Complimentary Romance Tropes and Paranormal Subgenres: Action and Adventure, Divine Intervention, Fairytale Retelling, Found Family, Mafia, Secret Royalty, Shape Shifters, Urban Fantasy, Vampires, Werewolves, Zodiac.

NOTES:

THEME OR SUBGENRE ~ DRAGONS ~

MISTAKEN THIEF

The Meet Cute setup: MC1 is walking home from work when they are accosted by dragon shifter MC2 demanding they return what they stole from a disreputable shady kingpin.

MC1, frightened out of their wits, assures MC2 that they have the wrong person.

Having intel on the thief, MC2 is suspicious because MC1 is a dead-ringer, but after snooping through their belongings they conclude that MC1 is telling the truth.

About to leave, a third party tries to kidnap MC1, forcing MC2 to intervene and save this unlucky lookalike.

Who is the true culprit? MC1's long-lost twin? Or an ex-friend trying to frame them for revenge?

No matter the mystery, one thing is for sure, MC1 won't be able to resist their attraction for their dragon protector forever...

Suggested Paranormal Genre/Subgenre: Dragons

Suggested Classic Romance Trope(s): Bodyguard/Military, Fish-Out-of-Water, Grumpy Sunshine, Instalove, Opposites Attract, Romantic Suspense.

Complimentary Romance Tropes and Paranormal Subgenres: Action and Adventure, Bounty Hunter, Bully Romance, Found Family, Mafia, Urban Fantasy.

NOTES:

NEED A LIGHT?

The Meet Cute setup: MC1 is about to give up cigarettes for good after this last one, but the problem is they just dropped their lighter down the drain.

When they ask handsome stranger MC2 for a light, they didn't expect them to click their fingers and emit a blue flame.

They also didn't expect their eyes to smolder in a way that makes them forget their cigarette altogether until MC2 has long disappeared into the night and their fingers get burned by the disappearing cigarette butt. It's no loss now, MC1 has found a new obsession and they won't rest until they find out who this mysterious stranger is.

Suggested Paranormal Genre/Subgenre: Dragons

Suggested Classic Romance Trope(s): Instalove, Opposites Attract, Romantic Suspense, RomCom.

Complimentary Romance Tropes and Paranormal Subgenres: Action and Adventure, Aliens, Angels, Bounty Hunter, Christmas, Curses, Cyborgs, Dark Romance, Deities, Demons and Devils, GameLit, Genie in a Bottle, Ghosts, Immortals, Mythical Creatures, Portal, Psychic Powers, Science-Fiction Romance, Urban Fantasy, Vampires, Werewolves, Witches/Wizards, Zodiac.

NOTES:

NEVER WAKE A SLEEPING DRAGON

The Meet Cute setup: Barista MC1 is closing up shop at the end of the day when they find a sleeping patron tucked away in a booth. They wake dragon MC2 to find themselves on the receiving end of MC2's violent fight-or-flight response!

MC2 barely manages to control themselves in time and gruffly tells off MC1, but then gathers their wits and apologizes for the imposition.

MC1 realizes that despite MC2's killer outfit (dragons are vain, after all) they don't have a place to sleep that night. Only intending to offer to make a call to a local homeless shelter, instead, MC1 invites the mysterious stranger to stay at their home.

Were they hypnotized by the heat in MC2's eyes or just tongue-tied at the burning attraction deep in their stomach? Little does MC1 know, they are inviting a whole lot of trouble into their lives because MC2 is on the run!

Mix it up: What if instead of a dragon, MC2 is a Vampire or Werewolf or Time traveler?

Suggested Paranormal Genre/Subgenre: Dragons

Suggested Classic Romance Trope(s): Bodyguard/Military, Forced Proximity, Opposites Attract, Romantic Suspense.

Complimentary Romance Tropes and Paranormal Subgenres: Action and Adventure, Bounty Hunter, Christmas, Curses, Destiny, Divine Intervention, Fairytale Retelling, Fated Mates, Found Family, GameLit, Revenge, Science-Fiction Romance, Seasonal, Shape Shifters, Time Travel, Urban Fantasy, Vampires, Werewolves, Witches/Wizards, Zodiac.

NOTES:

ROYAL DRAGON

The Meet Cute setup: MC1 is a royal dragon prince in need of an equally royal spouse! At least, that is what their mother says... Dragon shifter bloodlines need to be preserved, after all.

MC1 has rejected a slew of prospective partners, but when they are set up with a perfect-on-paper but equally engagement-hesitant royal counterpart MC2, they might have met their match–or better, an ally.

With both determined to keep their freedom, could a fake relationship and a perpetually long engagement provide the liberty and independence they both desire? Or will they fall in love despite both their best efforts?

Further considerations: What kind of character balance will give these two a spark at first sight? Will MC2 be a rowdy mess that makes MC1 laugh? A devious sneakster that gains MC1's respect and intrigue? Or a rare example of kindness and understanding in a world dominated by proud and prickly shifters obsessed with wealth and status?

Suggested Paranormal Genre/Subgenre: Dragons

Suggested Classic Romance Trope(s): Fake Dating, Marriage of Convenience, Opposites Attract, RomCom, Royalty.

Complimentary Romance Tropes and Paranormal Subgenres: Arranged Marriage, Blind Date, Christmas, Curses, Destiny, Divine Intervention, Fairytale Retelling, Historical, Immortals, Mythical Creatures, Seasonal, Shape Shifters, Soul Mates.

NOTES:

~ FAE ~

BETROTHED TO THE FAE

The Meet Cute setup: A deal was made, and now the fae has come to collect. MC1 finds themselves in an arranged marriage to Fae MC2, but will the Fae world provide more opportunities for happiness than their regular life offers?

With the fae's reputation for deception and rule twisting, can MC1 outsmart MC2 and secure themselves both a better deal as well as MC2's affection and devotion?

Mix it up: What if MC1 is standing in for the real debtor? What would motivate them to take their place? Money? Loyalty? Revenge?

Suggested Paranormal Genre/Subgenre: Fantasy Romance.

Suggested Classic Romance Trope(s): Cinderella, Fake Dating, Fish-out-of-water, Marriage of Convenience, Royalty.

Complimentary Romance Tropes and Paranormal Subgenres: Arranged Marriage, Blind Date, Christmas, Curses, Destiny, Divine Intervention, Dragons, Fae, Fairytale Retelling, Mythical Creatures, Portal, Seasonal, Secret Royalty.

NOTES:

THEME OR SUBGENRE ~ FAE ~

BLUE CAP BLUES

The Meet Cute setup: In a blended fae/human world, MC1 is a human lawyer trying to make partner with their fae boss MC2, who is giving them a run for their money with this new case: organizing a union for the Blue Caps, a hardworking type of pixie who do work and expect the median wage–no less and no more.

The last thing the Blue Caps want is MC1's assistance, but MC1 figures at least they haven't been set to work defending the far more bloodthirsty Red Caps.

Will MC1 be able to gain MC2's respect if they can't fulfill the brief? Or will MC2 finally be forced into admitting they've loved MC1 all along but fear what being partners in every sense but the one they desire means for their sanity...

Suggested Paranormal Genre/Subgenre: Fantasy Romance.

Suggested Classic Romance Trope(s): Alpha, Billionaire, Mafia, Forced Proximity, Romantic Suspense, RomCom.

Complimentary Romance Tropes and Paranormal Subgenres: Christmas, Curses, Dark Romance, Destiny, Divine Intervention, Fae, Fairytale Retelling, Mythical Creatures, Seasonal, Single Parent, Urban Fantasy.

NOTES:

CHANGELING

The Meet Cute setup: MC1 always thought they were a regular human, although one with a slightly unique appearance. But when their magical abilities emerge and sexy fae MC2 pushes them through a portal to an Elven realm, they realize they were switched at birth.

Will they choose the Fae world or the human world? Why did the fae queen order MC1 to be left with the humans in the first place, and how will they earn their place in fae society? Is MC2 to be trusted, or just another spy?

Mix it up: What if MC2 is a bounty hunter?

Suggested Paranormal Genre/Subgenre: Fantasy Romance.

Suggested Classic Romance Trope(s): Fish-out-of-water, Forced Proximity, Opposites Attract.

Complimentary Romance Tropes and Paranormal Subgenres: Bounty Hunter, Fated Mates, Found Family, Portal, Royalty, Urban Fantasy.

NOTES:

THEME OR SUBGENRE ~ FAE ~

FAE IN THE FAMILY

The Meet Cute setup: In the weirdest cross-cultural exchange ever, MC1's family takes in a foreign exchange student MC2 from the realm of the fae.

Can MC1 get along with Fae MC2 when they're mischievously messing with their stuff and invading their personal space by inspecting their toothbrush and underwear drawer?

MC2 might regret their antagonistic first impression when they start falling for their newfound frenemy. The opportunity for a sequel abounds when the year is up, and MC1 decides they want to try the exchange program in the other direction.

Suggested Paranormal Genre/Subgenre: Fantasy Romance.

Suggested Classic Romance Trope(s): Enemies to Lovers, Forced Proximity, RomCom, Royalty.

Complimentary Romance Tropes and Paranormal Subgenres: Academy, Bully Romance, Destiny, Divine Intervention, Fae, Fairytale Retelling.

NOTES:

THEME OR SUBGENRE ~ FAE ~

FALLING FOR THE FAIRY GODMOTHER

The Meet Cute setup: While trying to get to the Prince's Ball, Cinderella MC1 finds out they have a fairy godmother. But they never expected their Fairy Helper to be this dreamy or this grumpy!

MC2 informs them that the term 'fairy godmother' is a bit of a misnomer and that fae are assigned to assist certain humans in payment for something that happened generations ago–in effect, MC2 is bonded to a sentence of servitude, and MC1 is their warden!

As MC1 and MC2 get to know each other, will they get past their differences as MC1 falls out of love with their not-so-charming prince and much more deeply in love with their feisty Fae?

Suggested Paranormal Genre/Subgenre: Fantasy Romance.

Suggested Classic Romance Trope(s): Alpha, Cinderella, Grumpy Sunshine, Fake Dating, Forced Proximity, Opposites Attract, Royalty.

Complimentary Romance Tropes and Paranormal Subgenres: Blind Date, Bully Romance, Destiny, Divine Intervention, Fae, Fairytale Retelling, Fated Mates, Mythical Creatures, Science-Fiction Romance, Urban Fantasy..

NOTES:

~ GAME LIT & LITRPG ~

AI NPC SPOUSE

The Meet Cute setup: When MC1 died and went to heaven, they didn't expect to end up inside their favorite video game–but at least they know the rules: Farm the cabbages, kill the slimes, and marry an NPC so they can carry your stuff.

But when NPCSpouse MC2 alters their script, MC1 realizes the rules have changed. Sentient AI NPCs mean there's the possibility for a relationship more real than they'd ever hoped for... but an unpredictable game also means unpredictable threats!

Will MC1 and MC2 be able to unravel the mystery of this world together? And if code can be altered, high on MC1's list of priorities is to find a patch to let them remove their clothes. Because... uh... the default straw hat they were assigned is dorky. Yes. That's it. That's totally it.

Suggested Paranormal Genre/Subgenre: GameLit & LitRPG

Suggested Classic Romance Trope(s): Fake Dating, Forced Proximity, RomCom.

Complimentary Romance Tropes and Paranormal Subgenres: Angels, Arranged Marriage, Cyborgs, Destiny, Divine Intervention, GameLit, LitRPG, Science-Fiction Romance.

NOTES:

THEME OR SUBGENRE ~ GAME LIT & LITRPG ~

APOCALYPTIC ADVENTURER

The Meet Cute setup: Gamer Best Buds MC1 and MC2 find themselves transported into their favorite game–an apocalyptic digital land where the odds of survival are bleak.

Can they find a way to rebuild? Can they uncover the evil resource-hoarding plot that has kept the backwaters uninhabitable? And when life is finally sustainable, can MC1 convince MC2 to stop trying to save the world and settle down? The future of humanity relies on next gen kids after all.

Suggested Paranormal Genre/Subgenre: GameLit & LitRPG

Suggested Classic Romance Trope(s): Friends to Lovers.

Complimentary Romance Tropes and Paranormal Subgenres: Portal, Science Fiction Romance..

NOTES:

THEME OR SUBGENRE ~ GAME LIT & LITRPG ~

DUNGEON BEAST HAREM COLLECTOR

The Meet Cute setup: New Dates Unlocked! Each time Player MC1 delves into the dungeons, there are new monsters to slay and new bosses to... tame? With each new dungeon level achieved it becomes harder and harder for MC1 to leave their increasingly crowded little farmhouse, but they simply must know what will happen when they reach the final level!

With each new boss giving one extra clue, MC1 is only just finding out what kind of a game they're playing and that the stakes of losing are incredibly high.

Further considerations: What are the stakes of losing and how many lives have they burned through already? When they die for good, will they become one of the monsters? Or an unlockable boss for a future player to enslave? Will this realization alter the way they relate to their harem? How would this impact the way you write the other characters?

Suggested Paranormal Genre/Subgenre: GameLit & LitRPG

Suggested Classic Romance Trope(s): Alpha, Enemies to Lovers, Forced Proximity.

Complimentary Romance Tropes and Paranormal Subgenres: Action and Adventure, Arranged Marriage, Found Family, GameLit, Harem/Reverse Harem, Historical, LitRPG, Monster Romance, Mythical Creatures, Portal, Science-Fiction Romance.

NOTES:

FOREVER FARMING

The Meet Cute setup: MC1 trades in their human life to enter the digital world forever. Their choice of world? A slow paced cozy farming sim... But can they keep on grinding forever when they fall for townsfolk NPC MC2? How far can they level up their relationship?

Suggested Paranormal Genre/Subgenre: GameLit & LitRPG

Suggested Classic Romance Trope(s): Age Gap, Fake Dating, Forced Proximity, Friends to Lovers.

Complimentary Romance Tropes and Paranormal Subgenres: Action and Adventure, Found Family, GameLit, Harem/Reverse Harem, LitRPG, Portal, Science-Fiction Romance.

NOTES:

THEME OR SUBGENRE ~ GAME LIT & LITRPG ~

I TOOK AN ARROW TO THE KNEE

The Meet Cute setup: NPC MC1 was an adventurer once, but then they took an arrow to the knee...

In a sandbox RPG game like this though, there's always a new way to play and a new town to settle in.

Will they fall for another NPC character or the main player who keeps messing up the storyline and just can't seem to beat the final boss?

Suggested Paranormal Genre/Subgenre: GameLit & LitRPG

Suggested Classic Romance Trope(s): Forced Proximity, Friends to Lovers, Grumpy Sunshine, Instalove, Marriage of Convenience, RomCom.

Complimentary Romance Tropes and Paranormal Subgenres: Action and Adventure, Portal, Science-Fiction Romance.

NOTES:

THEME OR SUBGENRE ~ GAME LIT & LITRPG ~

IMMERSIVE 'PLAYER' MANSION

The Meet Cute setup: MC1 inherits a billion-dollar gaming company and a mansion with a secret. Behind a hidden doorway, they discover an immersive Virtual Reality room with a knockout MC2 among a sentient AI harem.

Can MC1 build a real world out of the remains of another person's fantasy? And what will be the cost when they start changing the code?

Further considerations: With sentient AI characters, how much free will do they have and how much are they restricted by their code? How will you illustrate this? For example, by having MC2 call MC1 by their predecessor's name? How will they adapt, learn and change as the story and relationships develop?

Suggested Paranormal Genre/Subgenre: GameLit & LitRPG

Suggested Classic Romance Trope(s): Billionaire, Celebrity, Cinderella, Fake Dating, Forced Proximity, Friends to Lovers, Instalove, Marriage of Convenience.

Complimentary Romance Tropes and Paranormal Subgenres: Found Family, GameLit, Harem/Reverse Harem, LitRPG, Portal, Science-Fiction Romance.

NOTES:

PLAYER TWO

The Meet Cute setup: When MC1 finds themselves in an RPG video game the novelty wears off fast, especially when the NPCs keep recycling the same dry old scripts. But when another player, MC2, barrels into town, MC1 finds they're not alone!

Will their friendship crash when they realize they have very different play styles? Or will this be the start of a great new adventure together? One question remains... How will they divide up the loot?

Suggested Paranormal Genre/Subgenre: GameLit & LitRPG

Suggested Classic Romance Trope(s): Friends to Lovers.

Complimentary Romance Tropes and Paranormal Subgenres: Action and Adventure, Curses, Destiny, Divine Intervention, Found Family, GameLit, Portal, Science-Fiction Romance.

NOTES:

THEME OR SUBGENRE ~ GAME LIT & LITRPG ~

TRAPPED IN A DATING SIM

The Meet Cute setup: MC1 is trapped in a Dating Sim and not as the player!

Can they get player MC2's attention long enough to reveal their true identity and ask for help to break free? What if MC2 only plays in bursts on lunch breaks from work and in the evenings?

Can MC1 and MC2 learn to love each other in a two-dimensional world where neither is sure what is real?

Further considerations: What if MC1 is actually a sentient AI with emotions?

Suggested Paranormal Genre/Subgenre: GameLit & LitRPG

Suggested Classic Romance Trope(s): Fake Dating, Fish-out-of-water, Forced Proximity, Friends to Lovers, RomCom.

Complimentary Romance Tropes and Paranormal Subgenres: Action and Adventure, Curses, Destiny, Fairytale Retelling, Fated Mates, Found Family, GameLit, Harem/Reverse Harem, Portal, Science-Fiction Romance, Seasonal.

NOTES:

~ GHOSTS ~

HEARING VOICES

The Meet Cute setup: Hearing voices is never a good thing, especially when it's one particular voice–a troublesome ghost urging MC1 to help avenge them!

Bullied into helping appease the ghost, MC1 is led to MC2–the descendant of the ghost's former rival.

Will MC1 do as told and avenge the family honor by duping MC2 as part of the ghost's madcap schemes? Or can MC1 and MC2 work together and get rid of their ghostly third wheel?

Suggested Paranormal Genre/Subgenre: Paranormal Romance Ghosts

Suggested Classic Romance Trope(s): Forced Proximity, RomCom.

Complimentary Romance Tropes and Paranormal Subgenres: Christmas, Curses, Destiny, Divine Intervention, Found Family, Ghosts, Historical, Psychic Powers, Revenge, Science-Fiction Romance, Seasonal, Single Parent, Small Town.

NOTES:

THEME OR SUBGENRE ~ GHOSTS ~

I'LL WAIT FOR YOU

The Meet Cute setup: Historian MC1 is obsessed with MC2's ancient and unrequited love letters.

And it turns out, MC2 never moved on in life, and now a ghost, they are still waiting around for the love of their life...

How will MC1 react, seeing the person they've been obsessed over materialize before their eyes? Faint with shock? Think they're working too much and hallucinating?

But now MC2 has fallen in love all over again, this time for MC1.

Suggested Paranormal Genre/Subgenre: Paranormal Romance Ghosts

Suggested Classic Romance Trope(s): Age Gap, Forced Proximity, Friends to Lovers, RomCom.

Complimentary Romance Tropes and Paranormal Subgenres: Christmas, Curses, Destiny, Divine Intervention, Fairytale Retelling, Historical, Medieval, Portal, Regency, Revenge, Seasonal, Small Town, Soul Mates, Time Travel.

NOTES:

INCOMPETENT NECROMANCER

The Meet Cute setup: MC1 is trying out the dark arts, perhaps trying to bring a loved parent or dog back to life, or maybe they just wanted to talk to Edgar Allan Poe to get some help on a university history assignment directly from the source.

What they didn't expect was to raise MC2, their sexy but wise-cracking soon-to-be love interest, from the grave.

Now MC2 is alive (sort of) again, what if they don't want to go back?

Suggested Paranormal Genre/Subgenre: Paranormal Romance Ghosts

Suggested Classic Romance Trope(s): Fake Dating, Fish-out-of-water, Forced Proximity, Friends to Lovers, RomCom.

Complimentary Romance Tropes and Paranormal Subgenres: Academy, Demons and Devils, Ghosts, Mythical Creatures, Portal, Psychic Powers, Science-Fiction Romance, Steampunk, Urban Fantasy.

NOTES:

IT'S IN THE ECTOPLASM

The Meet Cute setup: Researcher MC1 is on the hunt for samples of the ghostly residue ectoplasm, to provide a scientific breakthrough to cure a disease close to MC1's heart.

On entering ghost MC2's infamously haunted house, MC2 gives them the famous cold welcome that has frozen every other ghost-hunter and wannabe paranormal explorer out.

But when MC2 discovers MC1's intention, their curiosity and empathy is engaged. MC2 has unlimited quantities of exactly what MC1 wants—can they come up with an arrangement? Can MC1 provide the means for MC2 to get out and see the world outside once more?

What will they discover about each other in the process, and can they have a real relationship when either wonders if the other truly cares or is just using them?

Further considerations: MC2's cause of death and prior experiences with humans while in their ghostly form will give them their basis for a justified mistrust of MC1. What will MC1 have to do to gain MC2's trust?

Suggested Paranormal Genre/Subgenre: Paranormal Romance Ghosts

Suggested Classic Romance Trope(s): Age Gap, Forced Proximity, Friends to Lovers, Opposites Attract, Romantic Suspense, RomCom, Second Chance Romance.

Complimentary Romance Tropes and Paranormal Subgenres: Action and Adventure, Christmas, Divine Intervention, Fairytale Retelling, Ghosts, Portal, Psychic Powers, Science-Fiction Romance, Seasonal, Urban Fantasy.

NOTES:

KISS OF DEATH

The Meet Cute setup: There's no experience quite like first love, but it ended in literal tragedy when MC1's crush was killed at age fourteen after their first kiss.

Unfortunately, despite outgrowing them years ago, MC1's ghost-crush never moved on and is still loitering, trying to mess up their love life and cause general haunting havoc.

MC1's patience is finally up, and they call in Exorcist MC2, who turns out to be an absolute dreamboat and everything MC1 could ever want.

Can they clear out the old to make room for the new? And will MC2 be the key to MC1 understanding how to train their medium powers to communicate with the dead more constructively?

Suggested Paranormal Genre/Subgenre: Paranormal Romance Ghosts

Suggested Classic Romance Trope(s): Forced Proximity, Friends to Lovers, Grumpy Sunshine, Second Chance Romance.

Complimentary Romance Tropes and Paranormal Subgenres: Christmas, Curses, Destiny, Psychic Powers, Science-Fiction Romance, Seasonal, Small Town, Soul Mates, Steampunk, Urban Fantasy.

NOTES:

MISTAKEN KILLER

The Meet Cute setup: Murder Victim Ghost MC1 is out for revenge–on the wrong person!--and trashes MC2's apartment, making them late for an important job interview!

Only when they realize MC2 isn't their murderer do they apologize and try to make it up to them by putting everything back in place.

While MC2 remains unemployed, and with a lot of free time, will they assist their ghostly roommate and investigate who killed them? But if MC1 was wrong about MC2's involvement, could they be wrong about being dead as well?

If their journey reunites MC1 with their body, there may be a happily ever after in this after all.

Suggested Paranormal Genre/Subgenre: Paranormal Romance Ghosts

Suggested Classic Romance Trope(s): Age Gap, Celebrity, Cinderella, Enemies to Lovers, Fake Dating, Fish-out-of-water, Forced Proximity, Friends to Lovers, RomCom, Second Chance Romance.

Complimentary Romance Tropes and Paranormal Subgenres: Action and Adventure, Christmas, Destiny, Divine Intervention, Psychic Powers, Science-Fiction Romance, Seasonal, Soul Mates, Time Travel, Urban Fantasy.

NOTES:

NEAR DEATH EXPERIENCE

The Meet Cute setup: MC1 has a near-death experience that leaves them a little closer to the afterlife and with the ability to see and talk to ghosts!

They suddenly realize that all those little things going wrong in their life have been because of a cheeky but good-looking ghostly MC2 who sheepishly apologizes.

Determined to improve MC2's karma and help them move on to the afterlife, MC1 goes about making amends with the other victims of MC2's hauntings, but during their time together falls in love.

Will either be willing to let the other go?

Suggested Paranormal Genre/Subgenre: Paranormal Romance Ghosts

Suggested Classic Romance Trope(s): Age Gap, Bodyguard/Military, Celebrity, Cinderella, Forced Proximity, Friends to Lovers, Instalove, RomCom.

Complimentary Romance Tropes and Paranormal Subgenres: Academy, Action and Adventure, Divine Intervention, GameLit, Genie in a Bottle, Ghosts, Psychic Powers, Science-Fiction Romance, Seasonal, Small Town, Soul Mates, Urban Fantasy..

NOTES:

SECOND CHANCES DATING AGENCY

The Meet Cute setup: When MC1 signed up with the Second Chances Dating Agency, they thought it was for divorcees, not ghosts who hadn't managed to have a satisfactory love life the first time around!

Outraged and assuming they're the victim of a cruel prank, MC1 is ready to walk out of this weird dating scenario until their date arrives, sparkly ghost MC2 who despite being dead, has a zeal for life rarely seen in the living!

Suggested Paranormal Genre/Subgenre: Paranormal Romance Ghosts

Suggested Classic Romance Trope(s): Grumpy Sunshine, Instalove.

Complimentary Romance Tropes and Paranormal Subgenres: Blind Date, Christmas, Divine Intervention, Fairytale Retelling, Seasonal, Single Parent, Small Town, Soul Mates, Valentine's Day.

NOTES:

THE GHOST THAT DIDN'T KNOW

The Meet Cute setup: MC1 moves into a new house only to meet the recently deceased MC2, who is convinced they're still alive and MC1 is trespassing!

From an initial anger and terror-filled screaming match, these two will need to learn to cohabitate the building peacefully, and MC1's attempts at exorcism will eventually fade into curiosity about MC2's life story and reasons for staying behind.

Can MC2's unique ghostly character provide the cure to MC1's loneliness? And when they realize they would rather prolong MC2's stay in this realm, how will they navigate the physical boundaries of falling for a non-corporeal entity?

Suggested Paranormal Genre/Subgenre: Paranormal Romance Ghosts

Suggested Classic Romance Trope(s): Enemies to Lovers, Forced Proximity, Grumpy Sunshine, Opposites Attract.

Complimentary Romance Tropes and Paranormal Subgenres: Christmas, Curses, Destiny, Divine Intervention, Found Family, Ghosts, Historical, Psychic Powers, Regency, Seasonal.

NOTES:

~ IMMORTALS ~

DANCE WITH DEATH

The Meet Cute setup: MC1 is a backup dancer trying to make it big, and auditioning for a TV dance competition is an opportunity they can't pass up.

Thrown together with partners at random, MC1 is pleasantly surprised by their mysterious partner. MC2 not only matches their skill, but puts them through their paces. But what happens when MC1 realizes that MC2 isn't quite human and is using magic to succeed?

Further Considerations: What is MC2's motivation? Are they the Grim Reaper in disguise, trying to understand humans and yearning for a taste of life after so long escorting them at their end of life? And how will MC1 take this deception and its impact on their own abilities and career?

Suggested Paranormal Genre/Subgenre: Paranormal Romance

Suggested Classic Romance Trope(s): Celebrity, Cinderella, Forced Proximity, Friends to Lovers, Instalove.

Complimentary Romance Tropes and Paranormal Subgenres: Action and Adventure, Dark Romance, Deities, Demons and Devils, Destiny, Divine Intervention, Dragons, Fae, Fairytale Retelling, Genie in a Bottle, Ghosts, Immortals, Monster Romance, Mythical Creatures, Secret Royalty, Shape Shifters, Urban Fantasy, Vampires, Werewolves, Witches/Wizards, Zodiac..

NOTES:

DREAMING OF THE SANDMAN

The Meet Cute setup: MC1 had always been a lucid dreamer, but what happens when things become real and their dream lover, MC2, turns out to be the mythical Sandman in the flesh?

How will they react when their dreams become physical and the boundaries between realities break down? What other things can they pull out of dreams into the real world?

Suggested Paranormal Genre/Subgenre: Paranormal Romance

Suggested Classic Romance Trope(s): Forced Proximity, Friends to Lovers, Grumpy Sunshine, Instalove, Marriage of Convenience.

Complimentary Romance Tropes and Paranormal Subgenres: Academy, Action and Adventure, Dark Romance, Deities, Fairytale Retelling, Immortals, Mythical Creatures, Portal, Psychic Powers.

NOTES:

ELIXIR OF LIFE

The Meet Cute setup: Immortal MC1 has kept the secret to their long life close to their chest for centuries, but when the main ingredient to their elixir of life catches the equivalent of the potato blight, they'll have to venture out into the world again if they want to find a solution.

On finding botanist MC2, they thought they might have found hope, but MC2 might teach them a thing or two they never knew about living.

Suggested Paranormal Genre/Subgenre: Paranormal Romance

Suggested Classic Romance Trope(s): Age Gap, Enemies to Lovers, Fake Dating, Fish-out-of-water, Forced Proximity, Friends to Lovers, Grumpy Sunshine, Instalove, Romantic Suspense, RomCom.

Complimentary Romance Tropes and Paranormal Subgenres: Christmas, Curses, Cyborgs, Destiny, Divine Intervention, Fairytale Retelling, GameLit, Genie in a Bottle, Immortals, Medical Romance, Medieval, Science-Fiction Romance, Seasonal, Steampunk, Superpowers, Urban Fantasy.

NOTES:

IMMORTAL RECOGNIZED

The Meet Cute setup: Historian MC1 figures out the long-lived identity of Immortal MC2 after coming across their photos that date back several decades with no sign of aging.

How can MC1 convince them that it is safe to stop running?

Suggested Paranormal Genre/Subgenre: Paranormal Romance

Suggested Classic Romance Trope(s): Age Gap, Forced Proximity, Friends to Lovers.

Complimentary Romance Tropes and Paranormal Subgenres: Academy, Action and Adventure, Christmas, Curses, Destiny, Fairytale Retelling, Historical, Immortals, Mythical Creatures, Single Parent, Small Town, Soul Mates.

NOTES:

IMMORTAL HUNTER

The Meet Cute setup: Innocent Bystander MC1 is caught in the middle as someone else recognizes Immortal MC2 and is hunting them.

Will MC1 have some hidden skills or talents of their own that could put the chase to the end for good and finally allow MC2 to settle down and have a Happily Ever After?

Mix it Up: What if MC2 was an Alien on the run?

Suggested Paranormal Genre/Subgenre: Paranormal Romance

Suggested Classic Romance Trope(s): Bodyguard/Military, Forced Proximity, Friends to Lovers, Instalove, Romantic Suspense.

Complimentary Romance Tropes and Paranormal Subgenres: Action and Adventure, Aliens, Bounty Hunter, Destiny, Divine Intervention, Fairytale Retelling, GameLit, Immortals, Mythical Creatures, Portal, Science-Fiction Romance, Urban Fantasy..

NOTES:

SLEPT IN

The Meet Cute setup: Immortal MC1 gets woken up by MC2 after a long sleep. A really long sleep.

Were they frozen or imprisoned? How will MC1 react when they realize how many years have passed, and does MC2 have hidden intentions, or were they just at the right place at the right time?

Suggested Paranormal Genre/Subgenre: Paranormal Romance

Suggested Classic Romance Trope(s): Age Gap, Enemies to Lovers, Forced Proximity.

Complimentary Romance Tropes and Paranormal Subgenres: Academy, Action and Adventure, Curses, Divine Intervention, Fairytale Retelling, Genie in a Bottle, Ghosts, Historical, Immortals, Kidnapping, Urban Fantasy, Witches/ Wizards, Zodiac.

NOTES:

THEME OR SUBGENRE

~MONSTERS & MYTHICAL CREATURES~

BLIND DATE WITH A BEAST

The Meet Cute setup: It's hard to find love when you look like a Gorgon mated with a Minotaur. Especially if a Gorgon did mate with a Minotaur and MC1 was the result.

Enter the Blind Date with a Monster version of Tinder, where beasts get their chance at true love with those poor unfortunate souls who didn't think twice when they said on their profiles that personality mattered more than looks.

After dealing with anxiety issues that has seen them climb out windows on the last ten first dates, MC2 has made themself a promise: to see the next date through to the end...

Maybe these two will find true love if they can get past first impressions and take control of their instincts.

Suggested Paranormal Genre/Subgenre: Fantasy Romance

Suggested Classic Romance Trope(s): Age Gap, Celebrity, Cinderella, Fake Dating, Marriage of Convenience, Opposites Attract.

Complimentary Romance Tropes and Paranormal Subgenres: Blind Date, Christmas, Curses, Dark Romance, Destiny, Fairytale Retelling, Fated Mates, Kidnapping, LitRPG, Mafia, Monster Romance, Mythical Creatures.

NOTES:

THEME OR SUBGENRE ~ MONSTERS AND MYTHICAL CREATURES ~

GENIE IN A BOTTLE

Meet Cute setup: MC1 accidentally releases a genie in a bottle while cleaning out the attic of the old house they bought on the outskirts of town.

And while they never intended to use their wishes–knowing the troublesome reputation genies have for twisting the wording of wishes–when trouble crops up at work and life, genie MC2 provides a surprisingly good sounding board.

In the past few thousand years they've seen just about it all. What they never thought they'd see, however, was the day they'd fall in love–especially with a human.

Further considerations: With one MC effectively a captive, can they really be in love? Perhaps MC1 will need to give genie MC2 the freedom of the final wish for them to turn themselves human and begin a romance on equal footing...

Suggested Paranormal Genre/Subgenre: Fantasy Romance

Suggested Classic Romance Trope(s): Age Gap, Forced Proximity.

Complimentary Romance Tropes and Paranormal Subgenres: Christmas, Curses, Destiny, Divine Intervention, Fairytale Retelling, Found Family, GameLit, Genie in a Bottle, Ghosts, Immortals, Mythical Creatures, Portal, Seasonal, Urban Fantasy.

NOTES:

THEME OR SUBGENRE ~ MONSTERS AND MYTHICAL CREATURES ~

MEETING WITH MEDUSA

The Meet Cute setup: Gorgon MC1 has a difficult time dating when all their suitors end up petrified under their stony glare, and everyone thinks of them as a monster.

But when passerby MC2 has an accident, MC1 runs to the rescue, carefully caring for them without making eye contact.

MC2 falls deep in Instalove, but they are going to have to come up with creative solutions if neither wants to end up heartbroken or dead.

Further considerations: How could the gorgon's power be subverted? What if MC2 was temporarily blinded by the accident?

Suggested Paranormal Genre/Subgenre: Fantasy Romance

Suggested Classic Romance Trope(s): Instalove.

Complimentary Romance Tropes and Paranormal Subgenres: Blind Date, Christmas, Curses, Destiny, Divine Intervention, Fairytale Retelling, Fated Mates, Immortals, Mythical Creatures.

NOTES:

THEME OR SUBGENRE ~ MONSTERS AND MYTHICAL CREATURES ~

PHOENIX AND THE FIREMAN

The Meet Cute setup: In a world where Phoenix-kind changed their forms a thousand years ago to camouflage in the human world, Phoenix MC1 finds themselves trapped in a burning building–perhaps an animal shelter where they are carefully evacuating puppies by pushing them through a low window and out into the street.

Fireman MC2 isn't to know MC1 isn't in any real danger, but when they risk their life to save MC1, they've proven their character is brave and selfless: something Phoenix's find irresistible.

When Fireman MC2's breathing apparatus fails, it is Phoenix MC1 who drags them out of the building and provides healing with their magical tears.

Further considerations: When creatures have overpowered abilities, remember they should always come with a cost. If a Phoenix could cure any disease, why would they not? Would the act of curing pass the pain onto them? There needs to be a reason for the rarity of a Phoenix's tears.

Suggested Paranormal Genre/Subgenre: Fantasy Romance

Suggested Classic Romance Trope(s): Age Gap, Alpha, Fish-out-of-water, Forced Proximity, Friends to Lovers, Grumpy Sunshine, Instalove.

Complimentary Romance Tropes and Paranormal Subgenres: Action and Adventure, Christmas, Curses, Divine Intervention, Fairytale Retelling, Fated Mates, Found Family, GameLit, Monster Romance, Mythical Creatures.

NOTES:

THEME OR SUBGENRE ~ MONSTERS AND MYTHICAL CREATURES ~

SIREN SONG

The Meet Cute setup: Music producer MC1 hears Siren MC2 singing and is entranced!

Siren MC2 is hesitant to sing in public, knowing their powers of hypnotism could cause all manner of problems, but MC1 convinces them that their voice is something of beauty to share with the world.

Will MC2 give celebrity life a chance? And when MC1's boss wants to take advantage of MC2's ability, what will MC1 sacrifice to keep their siren safe?

Suggested Paranormal Genre/Subgenre: Fantasy Romance

Suggested Classic Romance Trope(s): Celebrity.

Complimentary Romance Tropes and Paranormal Subgenres: Christmas, Curses, Dark Romance, Divine Intervention, Fairytale Retelling, Monster Romance, Mythical Creatures, Science-Fiction Romance, Seasonal, Urban Fantasy, Valentine's Day.

NOTES:

~ PORTALS AND TELEPORTATION ~

POCKET DIMENSION PRISON

The Meet Cute setup: Pocket Dimensions are handy things for witches and wizards. Always bigger on the inside, they've been used to create rooms, dungeons or dresses with limitless pockets. But when trainee mage MC1 conjures one and accidentally falls into it with MC2, will they be able to figure their way out?

Further considerations: Being trapped within an elevator would be preferable to a pocket dimension because at least then they would know the fire brigade could be on their way! What skills could MC2 have that could help figure out this puzzle? And is MC1 the last person they want to be trapped with or the person they have been secretly crushing on?

Suggested Paranormal Genre/Subgenre: Witches

Suggested Classic Romance Trope(s): Forced Proximity, Grumpy Sunshine, Friends to Lovers.

Complimentary Romance Tropes and Paranormal Subgenres: Academy, Action and Adventure, Christmas, Curses, Destiny, Divine Intervention, Fairytale Retelling, GameLit, Genie in a Bottle, Portal, Science-Fiction Romance, Seasonal, Steampunk, Urban Fantasy, Vacation, Valentine's Day, Witches/Wizards.

NOTES:

THEME OR SUBGENRE ~ PORTALS AND TELEPORTATION ~

SUMMONING/BANISHING MISHAP

The Meet Cute setup: The problem with summoning and banishing objects is that when they appear, they need to come from somewhere, and when they disappear they need somewhere to go.

Young MC1 never figured that out when they were banishing their vegetables, and Young MC2 could never figure out why more kept appearing on their plate.

Years later, MC1 only realizes the connection when they summon something precious out of thin air, and it has a name scrawled across it. When they track their counterpart down, how will MC2 react? As well as having their treasure stolen, can they get past the trauma of years worth of double-broccoli to accept their soulmate?

Suggested Paranormal Genre/Subgenre: Fantasy Romance

Suggested Classic Romance Trope(s): Enemies to Lovers, Second Chance Romance.

Complimentary Romance Tropes and Paranormal Subgenres: Academy, Action and Adventure, Destiny, Fated Mates, Portal, Science-Fiction Romance, Seasonal, Secret Baby, Secret Royalty, Soul Mates, Steampunk, Urban Fantasy.

NOTES:

THEME OR SUBGENRE ~ PORTALS AND TELEPORTATION ~

TELEPORTATION MISHAP

The Meet Cute setup: MC1 suddenly develops the magical ability to teleport! Only they can not control when it occurs or the destination. Instead, they keep dropping out of the middle of whatever they were doing to land at the feet of the crush, MC2!

How does MC1 react? Are they awkward and embarrassed? Or cool? Do they devise a clever cover story for this seemingly random affliction?

And what happens when MC1 finds out they aren't teleporting themselves, but actually, MC2 is accidentally, or deliberately, summoning them?

Suggested Paranormal Genre/Subgenre: Fantasy Romance.

Suggested Classic Romance Trope(s): Fish-out-of-water, Forced Proximity,.

Complimentary Romance Tropes and Paranormal Subgenres: Academy, Action and Adventure, Christmas, Curses, Divine Intervention, Dragons, Fae, Fairytale Retelling, Fated Mates, GameLit, LitRPG, Portal, Psychic Powers, Science-Fiction Romance, Seasonal, Steampunk, Superpowers, Time Travel, Urban Fantasy.

NOTES:

THEME OR SUBGENRE ~ PORTALS AND TELEPORTATION ~

TIME WARP

The Meet Cute setup: Like many poor souls throughout history, Human MC1 stumbles into a fairy ring and is tempted to join the party where they fall for fae MC2… But what seems like only a couple hours in the fae realm is dozens of years in the human realm.

What happens when MC1 returns home to discover what they've lost? And when MC2 leaves the fae realm to follow them, will their Instalove last?

Will MC2 be able to find a way to return MC1 to the time they belong? Or will MC1 get past the idea of the grass being greener on the other side of the time shift and learn to love MC2 despite the cross-cultural and inter-dimensional barriers?

Suggested Paranormal Genre/Subgenre: Fantasy

Suggested Classic Romance Trope(s): Fish-out-of-water, Forced Proximity, Friends to Lovers, Instalove, Royalty, Second Chance Romance.

Complimentary Romance Tropes and Paranormal Subgenres: Academy, Curses, Cyborgs, Destiny, Fae, Fairytale Retelling, Mythical Creatures, Portal, Seasonal, Time Travel.

NOTES:

~ PSYCHIC POWERS AND MIND MAGIC ~

CONNECTED CONSCIOUS

The Meet Cute setup: MC1 thought it was just their inner voice/ conscience they were talking to. Until MC2 turns up in their life and they find themselves in sync and able to communicate via thought alone...

Mix it up: Forget a harmonious pairing. What if their paths crossing is a total disaster?

Think how such a bond could affect two people from opposite roles or social positions, for example, a police person and a thief, an adult student and university lecturer, or rival members of a gang or clan?

What chaos and conflict could a telepathic connection cause, and what effect would it have if one of them tried to shut it down completely?

Suggested Paranormal Genre/Subgenre: Science-Fiction Romance

Suggested Classic Romance Trope(s): Age Gap, Enemies to Lovers, Forced Proximity, Opposites Attract.

Complimentary Romance Tropes and Paranormal Subgenres: Academy, Action and Adventure, Aliens, Angels, Christmas, Curses, Destiny, Divine Intervention, Dragons, Fae, Fairytale Retelling, Fated Mates, GameLit, Portal, Psychic Powers, Seasonal, Steampunk, Superpowers, Time Travel.

NOTES:

THEME OR SUBGENRE ~ PSYCHIC POWERS AND MIND MAGIC ~

DREAMING OF YOU

The Meet Cute setup: MC1 has been dreaming of their future spouse since they were a kid. Picturing them, sketching them, imagining kissing them.

What happens when they meet MC2 face to face and realize they were not just a fantasy? And what happens when they realize that their dreams were not as private as they thought but were a connection the two of them shared?

A conscious connection could be a wonderful intimate experience, but if these two are in a taboo or inappropriate relationship, it could cause intense conflict.

Suggested Paranormal Genre/Subgenre: Science-Fiction Romance

Suggested Classic Romance Trope(s): Age Gap, Enemies to Lovers, Fake Dating, Forced Proximity.

Complimentary Romance Tropes and Paranormal Subgenres: Academy, Action and Adventure, Fated Mates, Harem/Reverse Harem, LitRPG, Monster Romance, Mythical Creatures, Portal, Psychic Powers, Seasonal, Secret Royalty, Shape Shifters, Soul Mates, Steampunk, Superpowers, Time Travel, Urban Fantasy.

NOTES:

THEME OR SUBGENRE ~ PSYCHIC POWERS AND MIND MAGIC ~

MIND SWAP

The Meet Cute setup: When MC1 offers themselves up as a volunteer at a hypnotist's magic show, they think their friends will have a laugh as they are forced to bark like a dog or something equally harmless and silly.

But MC2's hypnotism attempt backfires and swaps their consciousness with MC1!

What will these complete strangers discover to form a lasting and loving bond? And is the swap temporary or permanent?

Further Considerations: What would a location change do to this story? For example, is the magic show happening at a private party or fund-raising event? A Stag or Hen's night? Maybe it's part of a talent contest?

Suggested Paranormal Genre/Subgenre: Romantic Comedy

Suggested Classic Romance Trope(s): Celebrity, Cinderella, Fish-out-of-water, Forced Proximity, RomCom, Second Chance Romance.

Complimentary Romance Tropes and Paranormal Subgenres: Blind Date, Christmas, Curses, Divine Intervention, Fairytale Retelling, Fated Mates, Psychic Powers, Science-Fiction Romance, Seasonal.

NOTES:

THEME OR SUBGENRE ~ PSYCHIC POWERS AND MIND MAGIC ~

TELEPATHIC JOB INTERVIEW

The Meet Cute setup: MC1 has a reputation for being an HR whiz, but it's for a reason no one would expect: they can read minds.

This power gives them a supernatural edge in placing the right candidates in the right jobs. When they interview MC2, however, MC1 learns a surprising secret that sparks an intrigue that will throw both of their lives out of balance.

What could it be? Is it something touching, dangerous or outrightly weird? Is MC2 planning on robbing the business? Or looking to connect with their CEO birth parent? And now they know, will MC1 try to help or hinder these plans?

Further considerations: What is the job MC2 is interviewing for, and what are the stakes of them getting that job?

Suggested Paranormal Genre/Subgenre: Science-Fiction Romance

Suggested Classic Romance Trope(s): Alpha, Billionaire, Forced Proximity.

Complimentary Romance Tropes and Paranormal Subgenres: Destiny, Divine Intervention, Fairytale Retelling, Fated Mates, Found Family, GameLit, Psychic Powers, Seasonal, Soul Mates, Steampunk, Superpowers.

NOTES:

~ ROBOTS AND CYBORGS ~

MODEL MIX UP!

The Meet Cute setup: In the near future, MC1 opens up their Android box only to discover they've been sent the wrong model!

They were expecting a home help and health robot to keep the house clean and help with sick family members but they've been sent the super aggressive Security Model, MC2.

How will MC1 be able to train their Android MC2 to fulfill the tasks they wanted them to do? And what happens when MC2 develops or reveals they have a consciousness?

The line blurs between servant and friend as they become their confidant through ups and downs, but when attraction sparks can MC1 trust what robot MC2 feels, or are they just a slave to their programming?

Suggested Paranormal Genre/Subgenre: Science-Fiction Romance

Suggested Classic Romance Trope(s): Bodyguard/Military, Forced Proximity, Grumpy Sunshine, RomCom.

Complimentary Romance Tropes and Paranormal Subgenres: Action and Adventure, Christmas, Cyborgs, Destiny, Fairytale Retelling, LitRPG, Seasonal, Single Parent, Soul Mates, Steampunk.

NOTES:

STEAMPUNK PATCHWORK HEARTS

The Meet Cute setup: When MC1 suffered terrible injuries, they needed rebuilding from the base up. The cost of keeping their life 'ticking along' is that they are more machine than human.

Their confidence in their appearance shattered, they wonder if anyone will ever be able to see the heart within the Tin Can?

MC1's yearning question is answered when they need repairs and MC2, a mechanic with a heart of gold, comes along with just the gears needed to get their motor running.

Further Considerations: How would the characters change if you inverted their genders from how you first imagined? What would MC1's living situation and social life look like to make them feel the way they do when MC2 comes along? What has happened in MC2's past to make them empathize with the clockwork MC1?

Suggested Genre/Subgenre: Steampunk, Young Adult.

Suggested Classic Romance Trope(s): Cinderella, Fish-out-of-water, Forced Proximity, Friends to Lovers.

Complimentary Romance Tropes and Paranormal Subgenres: Christmas, Curses, Cyborgs, Divine Intervention, Found Family, GameLit, LitRPG, Monster Romance, Mythical Creatures, Science-Fiction Romance, Seasonal, Soul Mates, Steampunk, Superpowers, Urban Fantasy.

NOTES:

TIME TRAVEL CYBORG

The Meet Cute setup: Lonely-heart romantic MC1 was just trying to eat a microwave dinner and watch Pride and Prejudice (the BBC version) for the nth time when their party-for-one is crashed by a robot from the future!

When they manage to calm down, MC2 explains they've escaped their timeline and are hiding out in the past where they'll be safe from their life of slavery.

Can they trust MC1 to keep their cover? As they get to know each other, MC1's view of romance will change just as much as MC2's views of oppressive humans...

Suggested Paranormal Genre/Subgenre: Time Travel.

Suggested Classic Romance Trope(s): Cinderella, Friends to Lovers, Instalove, Marriage of Convenience, RomCom.

Complimentary Romance Tropes and Paranormal Subgenres: Christmas, Cyborgs, Destiny, Divine Intervention, Fairytale Retelling, GameLit, Historical, Immortals, Portal, Science-Fiction Romance, Seasonal, Steampunk.

NOTES:

THEME OR SUBGENRE

~ SHAPE SHIFTERS ~

BARE NAKED

The Meet Cute setup: When Hiker/Ranger MC1 finds Shifter MC2 naked and battered in the woods, they assume MC2 has been the victim of a wild animal as there have been several ferocious maulings in the forest as of late.

Luckily they have the first aid skills to patch MC2 together. But will they regret lending their assistance when they learn MC2's secret?

And who has been attacking the other hikers? Was it MC2 or the wild animal or shifter that injured MC2 in the first place?

Suggested Paranormal Genre/Subgenre: Werewolves and Shifters.

Suggested Classic Romance Trope(s): Bodyguard/Military, Forced Proximity, Friends to Lovers, Grumpy Sunshine, Instalove, Opposites Attract.

Complimentary Romance Tropes and Paranormal Subgenres: Action and Adventure, Christmas, Curses, Destiny, Fairytale Retelling, Fated Mates, Found Family, Mythical Creatures, Seasonal, Shape Shifters, Single Parent, Small Town, Soul Mates, Werewolves.

NOTES:

THEME OR SUBGENRE ~ SHAPE SHIFTERS ~

HIT AND RUN

The Meet Cute setup: MC1 accidentally hits an animal while driving. They rescue the poor creature from the side of the road and take them home to nurse back to health, little expecting the animal to turn into an attractive human MC2 in their bath overnight.

How does that discovery go the next morning? Is MC2 in a vulnerable position which makes them lash out? Or are they grateful for the attention and care? Is MC2 afraid that MC1 will reveal their secret?

Because MC1 caused the injury, how does that impact the relationship? Is MC2 known to MC1? A crush or a rival? The new person in town?

Suggested Paranormal Genre/Subgenre: Werewolves and Shifters.

Suggested Classic Romance Trope(s): Fish-out-of-water, Forced Proximity, Friends to Lovers, Romantic Suspense.

Complimentary Romance Tropes and Paranormal Subgenres: Action and Adventure, Aliens, Bounty Hunter, Bully Romance, Fated Mates, Found Family, Kidnapping, Medical Romance, Mythical Creatures, Seasonal, Secret Royalty, Shape Shifters, Single Parent, Small Town, Valentine's Day, Werewolves.

NOTES:

THEME OR SUBGENRE ~ SHAPE SHIFTERS ~

INJURED BEAR

The Meet Cute setup: Oh no! Bear shifter MC1 is caught in a bear trap! If they stay in their bear form, they may get caught by poachers and turned into a rug! But if they shift into their human form they may lose their hand or foot completely.

Just as they come to the hard but inevitable decision, they're discovered by the nature-loving, poacher-hating Ranger MC2, who has just the skills to save them.

MC1 will be sure to show their appreciation... that is, once the tranquillizer wears off.

Suggested Paranormal Genre/Subgenre: Werewolves and Shifters.

Suggested Classic Romance Trope(s): Alpha, Bodyguard/Military, Forced Proximity, Friends to Lovers.

Complimentary Romance Tropes and Paranormal Subgenres: Divine Intervention, Fairytale Retelling, Fated Mates, Found Family, Medical Romance, Medieval, Mythical Creatures, Seasonal, Shape Shifters, Single Parent, Small Town, Soul Mates, Zodiac.

NOTES:

MAMA BEAR

The Meet Cute setup: MC1 knows that universal truth that one should never, ever, under any circumstances, walk between a mama bear and her cubs.

Except, of course, if those cubs are in danger and by saving them MC1 wins the ferocious affection and loyalty of sexy mama shifter, MC2.

In that case, MC1 would advise that, yes, helping MC2 out was the best move they ever made.

Suggested Paranormal Genre/Subgenre: Werewolves and Shifters.

Suggested Classic Romance Trope(s): Bodyguard/Military, Enemies to Lovers, Fish-out-of-water, Forced Proximity, Friends to Lovers.

Complimentary Romance Tropes and Paranormal Subgenres: Found Family, Medical Romance, Science-Fiction Romance, Seasonal, Secret Royalty, Shape Shifters, Single Parent, Small Town, Soul Mates, Zodiac.

NOTES:

THEME OR SUBGENRE ~ SHAPE SHIFTERS ~

RAVEN

The Meet Cute setup: On a dark and stormy night, what will human MC1 do when raven shifter MC2 appears, tapping at their window?

Scream and shout and say "Nevermore"? Or let them in and out of the storm?

Suggested Paranormal Genre/Subgenre: Werewolves and Shifters.

Suggested Classic Romance Trope(s): Forced Proximity, Friends to Lovers, Instalove, Marriage of Convenience, Royalty, Second Chance Romance.

Complimentary Romance Tropes and Paranormal Subgenres: Academy, Arranged Marriage, Blind Date, Bounty Hunter, Christmas, Curses, Destiny, Fairytale Retelling, Fated Mates, Found Family, Mythical Creatures, Science-Fiction Romance, Seasonal, Shape Shifters, Small Town, Soul Mates, Steampunk, Zodiac.

NOTES:

RESEARCHER

The Meet Cute setup: Scorned by the scientific community, eccentric Researcher MC1 has spent years studying a rare animal they believe is linked to a race of shifters.

But Assistant/Guide/Historian and secret Shifter MC2 is determined to stop the research, so their race won't be revealed to the world and interferes with the findings.

Will Researcher MC1 put their heart before a career-defining discovery?

Suggested Paranormal Genre/Subgenre: Werewolves and Shifters.

Suggested Classic Romance Trope(s): Age Gap, Forced Proximity, Friends to Lovers, Grumpy Sunshine.

Complimentary Romance Tropes and Paranormal Subgenres: Academy, Action and Adventure, Bounty Hunter, Medical Romance, Mythical Creatures, Science-Fiction Romance, Seasonal, Shape Shifters, Single Parent, Zodiac.

NOTES:

SHACKING UP WITH GOLDILOCKS

The Meet Cute setup: Wandering MC1 finds a dilapidated shack in the woods and decides it would make a good base camp for their activities. Unfortunately, they are not as alone as they thought...

How will Bear Shifter MC2 react when they find MC1 has moved all their things, eaten all their food and is sleeping in their bed? MC2 would be angry if MC1 wasn't so gosh-darned cute.

Further considerations: Is your wandering MC1 a hiker, writer, scientist or general person looking for solitude after life became too much? How does their life situation impact the reason they are in the woods and what they are searching for?

Suggested Paranormal Genre/Subgenre: Werewolves and Shifters.

Suggested Classic Romance Trope(s): Forced Proximity.

Complimentary Romance Tropes and Paranormal Subgenres: Action and Adventure, Curses, Fairytale Retelling, Fated Mates, Found Family, Kidnapping, Mythical Creatures, Seasonal, Shape Shifters, Single Parent, Small Town, Soul Mates, Vacation, Zodiac.

NOTES:

SHARK!

The Meet Cute setup: When surfer MC1 gets separated from their board in the wake of a huge wave and gets saved by shark MC2 their views on the animal change forever.

But when they try to seek out their savior again, they bite off more than they can chew because one shark looks much like another!

Will shark-shifter MC2 be able to keep their not-shifter shark comrades under control?

And when MC2's shifter identity is revealed, can MC1 be the one to heal the broken heart that has had them avoiding land for so long?

Suggested Paranormal Genre/Subgenre: Mermaids.

Suggested Classic Romance Trope(s): Grumpy Sunshine, Instalove, Opposites Attract, Romantic Suspense, RomCom.

Complimentary Romance Tropes and Paranormal Subgenres: Action and Adventure, Christmas, Fated Mates, Found Family, Mythical Creatures, Science-Fiction Romance, Seasonal, Secret Royalty, Shape Shifters.

NOTES:

SHELTER FROM THE STORM

The Meet Cute setup: MC1 runs into bad weather while hiking and shelters in a cave, only to realize when they wake up in the night that they're not the only inhabitant! Shifter MC2, in their large animal predator form, has returned during the night!

MC1's initial fright calms when they realize they are not about to be eaten, and when their beast companion transforms into a hairy, sexy, bare-chested lumberjack they begin to think their streak of bad luck has come to an end.

Suggested Paranormal Genre/Subgenre: Werewolves and Shifters.

Suggested Classic Romance Trope(s): Age Gap, Alpha, Bodyguard/ Military, Forced Proximity, Grumpy Sunshine, Instalove, Second Chance Romance.

Complimentary Romance Tropes and Paranormal Subgenres: Action and Adventure, Bounty Hunter, Fated Mates, Found Family, Mythical Creatures, Seasonal, Shape Shifters, Zodiac.

NOTES:

THEME OR SUBGENRE ~ SHAPE SHIFTERS ~

TEDDY BEAR'S PICNIC

The Meet Cute setup: When unlucky-in-love Baker MC1 planned a romantic picnic with homemade bear claw pastries, they were not aware their blind date was gluten intolerant with a flair for the dramatic.

But when Bear Shifter MC2's nose picks up the delectable smell, they can't resist crashing the party! Blind Date runs screaming, and in the face of imminent death and the realization that they may have spent their final moments getting dumped again, MC1 decides that this hairy interloper is not getting two meals.

While MC2 stuffs their face with the picnic goodies, MC2 suddenly shifts to their human form and demands MC1 share the spoils. Struck dumb, MC1 drops the picnic basket as MC2 joins in as a stand-in date.

Suggested Paranormal Genre/Subgenre: Werewolves and Shifters.

Suggested Classic Romance Trope(s): Friends to Lovers, Grumpy Sunshine, Opposites Attract, Romcom.

Complimentary Romance Tropes and Paranormal Subgenres: Blind Date, Fairytale Retelling, Fated Mates, Mythical Creatures, Seasonal, Shape Shifters, Single Parent, Small Town, Valentine's Day.

NOTES:

~ SOUL MAGIC ~

BLOOD TIES

The Meet Cute setup: When MC1 and MC2 were kids, they swore a blood oath to each other that they would be together until the end of time. But life goes on, and when one of them moved towns, they lost track of each other.

But when MC1 starts dating after college, every prospective partner is cursed, and whenever lips touch they are met with disaster. There's only one thing to do–track down MC2 and demand a magical divorce. Naturally, MC2 has other ideas...

Further considerations: The parameters of the blood oath will be important for consistent rules for your plot.

What will the consequences of their oath be, and how will they try to subvert it? Can they ever truly be happy if they think their partner is with them only out of default because they can't be with anyone else? How can they be sure of their feelings? If they manage to break the oath but then still choose love, it will be much more satisfying than a relationship formed and maintained under duress.

Suggested Paranormal Genre/Subgenre: Fantasy Romance.

Suggested Classic Romance Trope(s): Second Chance Romance.

Complimentary Romance Tropes and Paranormal Subgenres: Academy, Arranged Marriage, Blind Date, Curses, Dark Romance, Fairytale Retelling, Science-Fiction Romance, Seasonal, Secret Baby, Soul Mates, Steampunk, Urban Fantasy, Witches/Wizards..

NOTES:

THEME OR SUBGENRE ~ SOUL MAGIC ~

KISS OF LIFE, SOUL MATE BIND

The Meet Cute setup: When learning CPR they should have told MC1 to never use it on a mage, or they'd end up binding their souls together for eternity.

But when grumpy alpha MC2 is in need of resuscitation, that's exactly what happens.

How will these two deal with their surprise connection?

Suggested Paranormal Genre/Subgenre: Witches.

Suggested Classic Romance Trope(s): Alpha, Cinderella, Grumpy Sunshine, Marriage of Convenience, Opposites Attract.

Complimentary Romance Tropes and Paranormal Subgenres: Curses, Destiny, Divine Intervention, Fairytale Retelling, Fated Mates, Psychic Powers, Science-Fiction Romance, Seasonal, Soul Mates, Urban Fantasy, Witches/Wizards, Zodiac.

NOTES:

THEME OR SUBGENRE ~ SOUL MAGIC ~

SOUL MATE AGENCY DUDS

The Meet Cute setup: In a world where everyone has their own soul mates and the code has been discovered to calculate compatibility, what happens when MC1 and MC2 are rejected from the system and informed they're destined to be alone forever?

Can they fake it 'till they make it? Or will they discover that love can be even stronger when it's a choice?

Suggested Paranormal Genre/Subgenre: Fantasy Romance

Suggested Classic Romance Trope(s): Fake Dating.

Complimentary Romance Tropes and Paranormal Subgenres: Academy, Arranged Marriage, Blind Date, Christmas, Dark Romance, Destiny, Fairytale Retelling, Fated Mates, Found Family, Science-Fiction Romance, Seasonal, Soul Mates, Steampunk, Valentine's Day.

NOTES:

~ SUPERPOWERS ~

ALONE NO LONGER

The Meet Cute setup: Moving town is nothing new to superhuman MC1. Since their youth, they have been forced to move once or twice a year due to the chaos they wreck with their secret abilities.

But when MC1 crosses paths with fellow superhuman MC2, they realize they're not the only one...

Can they build a Found Family with others of their kind who have a hidden community in this town? Or will the volatile nature of their powers keep them as an outcast in every corner of the world? When the prize is a normal life with MC2 by their side, it will be worth fighting for.

Further considerations: What kind of quirky or odd behaviors could you use to subtly demonstrate different abilities? A shifter might have a keen sense of smell even in their human form, what about someone with concealed wings? A person who can communicate with spirits or see auras? Do they have to hide behind sunglasses even at night? Draft out a few ideas based on your MC's characteristics and think about how they could influence the first meeting, especially if the one is trying to hide their powers.

Suggested Paranormal Genre/Subgenre: Superheroes

Suggested Classic Romance Trope(s): Forced Proximity, Friends to Lovers.

Complimentary Romance Tropes and Paranormal Subgenres: Academy, Action and Adventure, Found Family, GameLit, Mythical Creatures, Science-Fiction Romance, Shape Shifters, Small Town, Superpowers.

NOTES:

TOWN WITH SECRETS

The Meet Cute setup: Average-Joe-Type MC1 moves into a small town, but beneath the quaint charm the whole town feels slightly off, with oddities happening subtly in the background.

Upon meeting MC2 they fall in Instalove hard and their tunnel vision makes them forget all else, until they discover the town's secret. There is something in the water giving people special abilities.

Superhuman MC2 finds MC1's normality refreshingly attractive but worries about the consequences of dating an outsider. Worse, how will MC1 react when they realize their Instalove was brought on by MC2's chemically-altered super-charisma?

Further considerations: When a power impacts free will with abilities like instant attraction or mind magic, it is important to move slowly and have the benefitting character act with restraint if you want the reader to sympathize with them. If the superhuman is too opportunistic they can come across as a villain.

Suggested Paranormal Genre/Subgenre: Superheroes

Suggested Classic Romance Trope(s): Bodyguard/Military, Celebrity, Cinderella, Enemies to Lovers, Fake Dating, Instalove.

Complimentary Romance Tropes and Paranormal Subgenres: Academy, Action and Adventure, Bully Romance, Psychic Powers, Science-Fiction Romance, Shape Shifters, Small Town, Soul Mates, Steampunk, Superpowers, Time Travel, Urban Fantasy..

NOTES:

THEME OR SUBGENRE ~ SUPERPOWERS ~

UNTOUCHABLE

The Meet Cute setup: It's hard making friends when MC1's supernatural power means anyone who physically touches them will forget who they are. Trying to have a love life? Impossible.

But when MC2 tumbles into MC1 and is unaffected, it seems there is someone for everyone. It is just a pity MC2 hates MC1's guts.

Suggested Paranormal Genre/Subgenre: Superheroes

Complimentary Romance Tropes and Paranormal Subgenres: Enemies to Lovers, Grumpy Sunshine

Complimentary Romance Tropes and Paranormal Subgenres: Fairytale Retelling, Fated Mates, GameLit, Medical Romance, Science-Fiction Romance, Steampunk, Superpowers, Urban Fantasy, Witches/Wizards, Zodiac.

NOTES:

~TIME TRAVEL & TIME MANIPULATION~

APPRENTICE

The Meet Cute setup: Apprentices always mess things up when they're learning, but Rookie MC1 truly messes up when they try to bend time to see their crush, MC2, and inadvertently creates multiple timelines–all of which end in MC2's death!

Can MC1 hop across every timeline and weave them back together again before their Master/Supervisor learns they have broken time? And what if the first version of MC2 demands to come along for the ride across dimensions to ensure their survival?

After such an adventure and seeing the effort MC1 makes to ensure MC2 lives a long and happy life, with or without them, could MC2 choose anyone but the accident-prone MC1?

Further Considerations: To make this concept unique, consider the type of time travel being wielded. Is the origin magical or pure science fiction? What is this time manipulation used for? And what could go wrong when trying to learn each of those skills?

Suggested Paranormal Genre/Subgenre: Time Travel, Young Adult.

Suggested Classic Romance Trope(s): Fish-out-of-water, Romantic Suspense, RomCom, Second Chance Romance.

Complimentary Romance Tropes and Paranormal Subgenres: Academy, Action and Adventure, Curses, Fairytale Retelling, Fated Mates, Found Family, GameLit, Genie in a Bottle, Science-Fiction Romance, Soul Mates, Steampunk, Superpowers, Time Travel, Urban Fantasy, Zodiac.

NOTES:

THEME OR SUBGENRE ~ TIME TRAVEL AND TIME MANIPULATION ~

GATEWAY TO THE PAST

The Meet Cute setup: Present-day MC1 discovers a gateway to a fixed point in the past where they meet MC2, who charms them with their old-fashioned values and mannerisms.

Considerations: Other than the natural fish-out-of-water situation this setup lends itself toward, a conflict in time travel stories is the dilemma: stay or go?

Will MC1 decide they prefer to live in the Ye Olde Golden Era? Or will they risk bringing their historical love interest back to the present for the sake of modern medicines and conveniences?

Suggested Paranormal Genre/Subgenre: Time Travel

Suggested Classic Romance Trope(s): Fish-out-of-water, Forced Proximity.

Complimentary Romance Tropes and Paranormal Subgenres: Christmas, Destiny, Historical, Portal, Science-Fiction Romance, Time Travel, Urban Fantasy, Witches/Wizards, Zodiac.

NOTES:

THEME OR SUBGENRE ~ TIME TRAVEL AND TIME MANIPULATION ~

PAST MEETS PRESENT

The Meet Cute setup: A gateway from the past opens up. MC1 is whisked from the past and dumped into the present, right at MC2's feet!

What event was MC1 snatched away from, and will MC2 be able to assist them back to their own time? Or will they decide their destinies are better off together?

Further considerations: The context of when and why MC1 is transported from will affect how they act and their desire to return home.

Were they snatched right out of a battle they needed to win to save their people? Or were they a victim of their own curiosity, sifting through magical possessions of their arranged marriage partner who may or may not turn out to be an evil time-traveling witch or wizard themselves?

Suggested Paranormal Genre/Subgenre: Time Travel

Suggested Classic Romance Trope(s): Forced Proximity.

Complimentary Romance Tropes and Paranormal Subgenres: Historical, Portal, Science-Fiction Romance, Time Travel, Urban Fantasy, Witches/Wizards.

NOTES:

THEME OR SUBGENRE ~ TIME TRAVEL AND TIME MANIPULATION ~ REWIND TIME

The Meet Cute setup: MC1 has the ability to rewind time to do over moments again and again. How far back can MC1 rewind time? A minute? An hour or a day?

But more importantly, how will they use it to win MC2s heart?

If they made a terrible first impression, can they undo this? Or will they fail every time?

Maybe the effect of their ability wears off, or MC2 is the first person to be unaffected? Or will an accident occur, and they become stuck in a time loop? How will they figure out how to break the cycle?

Suggested Paranormal Genre/Subgenre: Time Travel

Suggested Classic Romance Trope(s): Romantic Suspense, RomCom, Second Chance Romance.

Complimentary Romance Tropes and Paranormal Subgenres: Academy, Action and Adventure, Fairytale Retelling, LitRPG, Portal, Psychic Powers, Science-Fiction Romance, Steampunk, Superpowers, Time Travel.

NOTES:

THEME OR SUBGENRE ~ TIME TRAVEL AND TIME MANIPULATION ~
TIME FREEZE

The Meet Cute setup: Time freezes suddenly for everyone else except MC1.

Do they use this time anomaly to spy on their crush, MC2? Or do they discover MC2 is also unaffected?

Who else is excluded from this time freeze? Why is it happening, and who is controlling it? One of the MCs or someone else?

Suggested Paranormal Genre/Subgenre: Time Travel

Suggested Classic Romance Trope(s): Fish-out-of-water.

Complimentary Romance Tropes and Paranormal Subgenres: Academy, Action and Adventure, Curses, Divine Intervention, Fairytale Retelling, Fated Mates, Found Family, GameLit, Portal, Psychic Powers, Science-Fiction Romance, Steampunk, Superpowers, Time Travel, Urban Fantasy.

NOTES:

~ VAMPIRES ~

BROUGHT TO THE VAMPIRE COURT

The Meet Cute setup: Human MC1 is abducted by one of Courtly Vampire MC2's servants and dumped at MC2's feet, but when face to face with certain death, MC2 has a change of heart.

Why? Perhaps MC1 resembles a long-lost love, or in the recent past, MC1 did them a significant favor. Either way, MC1 has escaped with their life but is now a prisoner until MC2 can be assured that their secret will not be spilled.

How will MC1 fit into a vampire court? And if they're ever released, will they be able to stay away when no human suitors live up to MC2's example?

Further considerations: The culture and hierarchy of the vampire's court can be blended with the time they originated from and modern influences that may have leaked in via human contact. Think about who the vampire was in life. What about their mannerism and character is so unique that would set them apart from every other suitor in MC1's life?

Suggested Paranormal Genre/Subgenre: Vampires.

Suggested Classic Romance Trope(s): Royalty.

Complimentary Romance Tropes and Paranormal Subgenres: Arranged Marriage, Bully Romance, Dark Romance, Harem/Reverse Harem, Immortals, Kidnapping, LitRPG, Mafia, Monster Romance, Mythical Creatures, Revenge, Secret Royalty, Shape Shifters, Vampires, Werewolves, Witches/Wizards, Zodiac.

NOTES:

FAILED FEEDING

The Meet Cute setup: Vampire MC1 tries to feed, but tough-cookie MC2 uses their ex-military skills and flips the situation from victim to vanquisher. What will MC2 do with MC1 at their mercy? And what can MC1 promise them to escape intact?

Further considerations: If MC1 is low in rank in a vampire clan, they may be limited in what they can promise. They may also have a rebellious streak and desire or need a human friend and confidant.

If MC1 is a lone vampire or higher up in the vampire clan hierarchy, they may be attracted to MC2's fighting ability and want to use them to increase their own strength and standing.

What would change about MC2's character and motivation depending on where they are situated in your world's vampire society?

Suggested Paranormal Genre/Subgenre: Vampires.

Suggested Classic Romance Trope(s): Bodyguard/Military, Enemies to Lovers, Fake Dating.

Complimentary Romance Tropes and Paranormal Subgenres: Action and Adventure, Dark Romance, Destiny, Fated Mates, Found Family, Harem/Reverse Harem, Kidnapping, Mafia, Secret Royalty, Shape Shifters, Urban Fantasy, Vampires, Werewolves, Witches/Wizards, Zodiac.

NOTES:

FAILED THRALL

The Meet Cute setup: Hypnotising slaves is nothing new to Vampire MC1, it's how they've functioned for hundreds of years. But when would-be victim MC2 is able to resist their mind powers, MC1 knows they've met someone special–perhaps they've even met their soulmate.

Further considerations: What if MC2 wasn't human? Or what if they weren't human, and didn't know it themselves?

Suggested Paranormal Genre/Subgenre: Vampires.

Suggested Classic Romance Trope(s): Age Gap, Alpha, Forced Proximity, Romantic Suspense.

Complimentary Romance Tropes and Paranormal Subgenres: Curses, Dark Romance, Fated Mates, Immortals, Kidnapping, LitRPG, Mafia, Secret Royalty, Shape Shifters, Soul Mates, Urban Fantasy, Vampires, Werewolves, Witches/ Wizards, Zodiac.

NOTES:

MEET ME AT MIDNIGHT

The Meet Cute setup: Historian/Academic/librarian human MC1 is doing some late-night shopping and comes across Vampire MC2 in the fresh meats section as they try to select the juiciest piece. After some unsolicited advice, MC2 changes their selection to the more iron-rich venison steak and human MC1 is oddly compelled to ditch the garlic from their basket.

MC1 discovers MC2 is an expert in exactly the period of history (of course they are, they lived through it after all) they are writing their PhD thesis on, and suggests coffee the next day, but there's a problem. Vampire MC2 can't go out during the day.

But with the promise of the best human interaction they've had in well over a decade, they suggest what turns into a series of midnight dates. How long will their romance trail on before MC1 discovers the truth?

Further considerations: How does the meet-cute location alter the vibe of the story? If your MCs meet in a nightclub or a gym, how do their motivations and reactions to each other change?

Suggested Paranormal Genre/Subgenre: Vampires.

Suggested Classic Romance Trope(s): Friends to Lovers, Instalove, Opposites Attract, Romcom.

Complimentary Romance Tropes and Paranormal Subgenres: Christmas, Curses, Destiny, Divine Intervention, Fairytale Retelling, Found Family, Historical, Immortals, Mythical Creatures, Seasonal, Shape Shifters, Single Parent, Small Town, Soul Mates, Valentine's Day, Vampires, Werewolves, Witches/Wizards, Zodiac.

NOTES:

ROYAL VAMPIRE

The Meet Cute setup: When MC1 accidentally saves Vampire Royalty MC2, they upset the balance of power. To save face with their court, MC2 decides the wisest course of action is to enter into a fake dating relationship.

MC1 agrees while trying to find a way to back out of it, but maybe along the way they realize being treated like undead royalty isn't so bad after all.

Suggested Paranormal Genre/Subgenre: Vampires.

Suggested Classic Romance Trope(s): Fake Dating, Royalty.

Complimentary Romance Tropes and Paranormal Subgenres: Found Family, Mafia, Monster Romance, Mythical Creatures, Seasonal, Secret Royalty, Single Parent, Small Town, Urban Fantasy, Vampires, Werewolves, Witches/Wizards, Zodiac.

NOTES:

SAVED BY DINNER

The Meet Cute setup: Vampire MC1 is about to feed on human MC2 and get a delicious vampire dinner...

Only before the fangs come out, a Vampire Hunter arrives to take MC1 down! Misunderstanding the situation, MC2 saves their would-be attacker, and now the wealthy and powerful vampire owes them a boon!

Suggested Paranormal Genre/Subgenre: Vampires.

Suggested Classic Romance Trope(s): Enemies to Lovers, Grumpy Sunshine.

Complimentary Romance Tropes and Paranormal Subgenres: Action and Adventure, Bounty Hunter, Christmas, Divine Intervention, Fairytale Retelling, Immortals, Mythical Creatures, Seasonal, Secret Royalty, Shape Shifters, Single Parent, Small Town, Urban Fantasy, Vacation, Valentine's Day, Vampires, Werewolves, Witches/Wizards, Zodiac.

NOTES:

SAVED BY THE VAMPIRE

The Meet Cute setup: Human MC1 is mugged on their way home from work! Vampire MC2 swoops in to save the day, sending the mugger running for the hills, and MC1 falls into Instalove hard.

Further considerations: Did the vampire save MC1 on purpose? This shows a noble side to an otherwise aloof character.

If the vampire MC was actually targeting the mugger for their meal and they saved MC1 as a happy coincidence, this may show a more opportunistic character... In which case, what is the reason they don't treat himself to a meal on MC1?

Thinking about the character's motivations can change the context and feel of this exchange.

Suggested Paranormal Genre/Subgenre: Vampires.

Suggested Classic Romance Trope(s): Instalove.

Complimentary Romance Tropes and Paranormal Subgenres: Dark Romance, Destiny, Divine Intervention, Fated Mates, Harem/Reverse Harem, Historical, Immortals, Monster Romance, Mythical Creatures, Seasonal, Small Town, Urban Fantasy, Vampires, Werewolves, Witches/Wizards, Zodiac.

NOTES:

VAMPIRE MAFIA

The Meet Cute setup: Rebel Without a Cause MC1 always thought they were the most dangerous thing on the streets until a petty crime goes wrong and they're caught up in the underground dealings of the Vampire Mafia.

Vampire MC2 convinces their fanged associates not to feast on MC1, so long as they remain useful as an underling. Will MC1 ever be able to earn a place in vampire society by MC2's side?

Suggested Paranormal Genre/Subgenre: Vampires.

Suggested Classic Romance Trope(s): Bodyguard/Military, Celebrity, Fish-out-of-water, Forced Proximity, Friends to Lovers, Grumpy Sunshine, Instalove, Romantic Suspense, RomCom, Royalty.

Complimentary Romance Tropes and Paranormal Subgenres: Action and Adventure, Bounty Hunter, Bully Romance, Dark Romance, Fated Mates, Harem/ Reverse Harem, Historical, Immortals, Mafia, Monster Romance, Mythical Creatures, Revenge, Secret Royalty, Shape Shifters, Urban Fantasy, Vampires, Werewolves, Witches/Wizards, Zodiac.

NOTES:

VEGAN VAMPIRE

The Meet Cute setup: Vegan vampire MC2 turns up at MC1's juice bar, relying solely on fresh beetroot juice to keep them going. Only MC1 is all out of beets and MC2 needs a drink! Will MC1 offer up their veins willingly, or will MC2's baser instincts overcome them followed by a heartfelt apology?

Suggested Paranormal Genre/Subgenre: Vampires.

Suggested Classic Romance Trope(s): Romcom.

Complimentary Romance Tropes and Paranormal Subgenres: Blind Date, Christmas, Divine Intervention, Fairytale Retelling, Immortals, Seasonal, Secret Royalty, Soul Mates, Urban Fantasy, Vampires, Werewolves, Witches/Wizards, Zodiac.

NOTES:

YOUR FRIENDLY NEIGHBOURHOOD VAMPIRE

The Meet Cute setup: Secret Vampire MC1 has had a crush on Single Parent MC2 ever since they moved into the neighborhood, but they've never had the confidence to approach them. But when a mugger attacks MC1 is straight to the rescue!

MC2 suddenly sees their spooky-loner neighbor in a brand new light, but will it last when they realize the secret MC1 has been hiding?

Suggested Paranormal Genre/Subgenre: Vampires.

Suggested Classic Romance Trope(s): Bodyguard/Military, Friends to Lovers.

Complimentary Romance Tropes and Paranormal Subgenres: Action and Adventure, Christmas, Fated Mates, Found Family, Seasonal, Shape Shifters, Single Parent, Small Town, Urban Fantasy, Vampires, Werewolves, Witches/Wizards, Zodiac.

NOTES:

~ WEREWOLVES ~

ACCIDENTAL IMPRINT

The Meet Cute setup: When on vacation Werewolf MC1 sees MC2 in medical trouble, they run to the rescue and resuscitate them with the kiss of life.

Unbeknownst to MC2, they have tied their fates together from the moment their lips touched.

How will MC1 explain their predicament, especially when MC2 is already engaged? MC1 and MC2 are about to discover that sometimes accidents happen for a reason.

Suggested Paranormal Genre/Subgenre: Werewolves and Shifters

Suggested Classic Romance Trope(s): Forced Proximity.

Complimentary Romance Tropes and Paranormal Subgenres: Action and Adventure, Divine Intervention, Fated Mates, Found Family, Medical Romance, Mythical Creatures, Psychic Powers, Seasonal, Shape Shifters, Single Parent, Small Town, Soul Mates, Urban Fantasy, Vacation, Werewolves, Witches/Wizards, Zodiac.

NOTES:

DATE WITH THE VET (BETA/OMEGA WOLF)

The Meet Cute setup: MC1 rushes a wounded animal into the local vet, MC2, who is a Secret Werewolf.

Moved by MC1's caring nature, they form a connection. MC2 thinks perhaps MC1 could understand and love them despite their lowly rank at the bottom of the pack hierarchy. Will MC1 provide the confidence boost MC2 needs to find their teeth and start clawing their way up in their society?

Further considerations: By introducing MC2 in a vet, or another carer role, the reader will see their soft and cuddly side before the wild side is revealed. Firmly establishing their nice side first will allow more aggressive behavior with other pack mates later in the story, with losing reader sympathy.

Suggested Paranormal Genre/Subgenre: Werewolves and Shifters

Suggested Classic Romance Trope(s): Age Gap, Bodyguard/Military, Celebrity, Forced Proximity, Friends to Lovers.

Complimentary Romance Tropes and Paranormal Subgenres: Action and Adventure, Arranged Marriage, Bounty Hunter, Christmas, Curses, Fairytale Retelling, Fated Mates, Found Family, Medical Romance, Mythical Creatures, Secret Royalty, Shape Shifters, Single Parent, Small Town, Soul Mates, Urban Fantasy, Vacation, Vampires, Werewolves, Witches/Wizards, Zodiac.

NOTES:

FATED MATES/IMPRINTED MATES

The Meet Cute setup: Human MC1's life is disrupted when Werewolf MC2 accosts them and informs them that their romance is written in the stars. MC1 rejects them on the spot, but their interest grows when they see how far MC2 will go to protect them and claim them as their own.

Further considerations: Figure out how the imprint system works in your universe. Is it fate, or was there an instance in the MCs' pasts that tied them together?

Was your human MC selected as a marriage candidate by the alpha wolf in a paranormal twist on an arranged marriage? How does this impact the relationship and the willingness of each party?

Suggested Paranormal Genre/Subgenre: Werewolves and Shifters

Suggested Classic Romance Trope(s): Enemies to Lovers, Fake Dating, Forced Proximity, Grumpy Sunshine, Royalty, Second Chance Romance.

Complimentary Romance Tropes and Paranormal Subgenres: Arranged Marriage, Blind Date, Curses, Fated Mates, Kidnapping, Monster Romance, Mythical Creatures, Portal, Psychic Powers, Seasonal, Secret Baby, Secret Royalty, Shape Shifters, Single Parent, Small Town, Soul Mates, Urban Fantasy, Valentine's Day, Vampires, Werewolves, Witches/Wizards, Zodiac.

NOTES:

FIRST DATE, INTERRUPTED

The Meet Cute setup: Their blind date goes horribly wrong when Werewolf MC1 after they lose control of their form, and an unsuspecting MC2 finds themselves with a large wolf instead of their date...

But what if MC2 has a secret too? Maybe they have an ability or skill that could be even more dangerous than lycanthropy.

Further considerations: Think about the venue for this date. How would changing into a werewolf during a church picnic affect the situation and tone of the story? What about a restaurant on Valentine's Day, an office party, or wedding?

Suggested Paranormal Genre/Subgenre: Werewolves and Shifters

Suggested Classic Romance Trope(s): Fake Dating, Fish-out-of-water, RomCom, Royalty, Second Chance Romance.

Complimentary Romance Tropes and Paranormal Subgenres: Academy, Action and Adventure, Blind Date, Curses, Divine Intervention, Fated Mates, Mythical Creatures, Seasonal, Secret Royalty, Shape Shifters, Single Parent, Small Town, Soul Mates, Superpowers, Time Travel, Urban Fantasy, Vacation, Valentine's Day, Vampires, Werewolves, Witches/Wizards, Zodiac.

NOTES:

LIVING WITH WOLVES

The Meet Cute setup: MC1 is lost in the woods in the middle of a storm and finds themselves surrounded by wolves!

Much to their surprise, their terror is misplaced as the wolves lead them to the safety of their cave until the storm passes. When daylight comes, MC1 is surrounded, not by a pack of predators, but by a group of werewolves living in isolation from humans.

Werewolf MC2 offers to escort them to a location where they can find their way out on the condition they never come back. But after this encounter, how could MC1 not return?

Suggested Paranormal Genre/Subgenre: Werewolves and Shifters

Suggested Classic Romance Trope(s): Age Gap, Alpha, Bodyguard/ Military, Forced Proximity.

Complimentary Romance Tropes and Paranormal Subgenres: Action and Adventure, Arranged Marriage, Blind Date, Dark Romance, Destiny, Divine Intervention, Fated Mates, Found Family, Harem/Reverse Harem, Mythical Creatures, Seasonal, Shape Shifters, Single Parent, Small Town, Soul Mates, Urban Fantasy, Vacation, Vampires, Werewolves, Witches/Wizards, Zodiac.

NOTES:

THEME OR SUBGENRE ~ WEREWOLVES ~

MY, WHAT BIG TEETH YOU HAVE

The Meet Cute setup: MC1 comes face to face with a wolf and is convinced this is the end... But Werewolf MC2 has enough control over their baser instincts that they turn and walk back into the shadows leaving MC1 with a sense of intrigue and curiosity.

Are these the same yellow eyes they have seen near their house every night for the last week?

Fear turns to affection, especially when MC1 finds MC2 injured in the woods in their human form–now it is their turn to show mercy and caring. And how long until they join the dots?

Suggested Paranormal Genre/Subgenre: Werewolves and Shifters

Suggested Classic Romance Trope(s): Bodyguard/Military, Forced Proximity, Friends to Lovers, Instalove.

Complimentary Romance Tropes and Paranormal Subgenres: Christmas, Curses, Dark Romance, Destiny, Divine Intervention, Fairytale Retelling, Fated Mates, Found Family, Medical Romance, Mythical Creatures, Psychic Powers, Seasonal, Shape Shifters, Single Parent, Small Town, Soul Mates, Urban Fantasy.

NOTES:

TEACHER'S PET

The Meet Cute setup: Teacher/Nanny MC1 finds themselves on the receiving end of werewolf MC2's intense stare when they are kidnapped!

When MC1 realizes they were kidnapped to help raise the wolfpack pups in desperate need of an education, they decide to stay, but that doesn't stop them from going head to head with MC2 on the way they've decided to lead the pack!

MC2 may have met their match with this strong-headed but caring teacher, and you just know they'll form an alpha pair to be feared.

Further considerations: With kidnapping tropes, no matter how desperate the reason for taking them, for the kidnapped MC to get a great happy ending, they need to have the freedom of choice to leave or to stay–which will make their decision to stay all the more satisfying to read.

To do this, there needs to be a power transition whereby the kidnap-victim becomes the more powerful party.

Suggested Paranormal Genre/Subgenre: Werewolves and Shifters

Suggested Classic Romance Trope(s): Alpha, Fish-out-of-water, Forced Proximity, Marriage of Convenience.

Complimentary Romance Tropes and Paranormal Subgenres: Arranged Marriage, Blind Date, Christmas, Fairytale Retelling, Fated Mates, Found Family, Kidnapping, Mythical Creatures, Portal, Psychic Powers, Seasonal, Secret Royalty, Shape Shifters, Single Parent, Small Town, Soul Mates, Urban Fantasy, Werewolves, Witches/Wizards, Zodiac.

NOTES:

UNWILLING IMPRINT

The Meet Cute setup: MC1 is forced into a werewolf lair where momentary relief they won't be eaten turns to shock on learning they are the fated-mate of Werewolf MC2.

But things get stranger when MC2 rejects them and refuses to consummate the relationship. Determined to be free of their fate, MC2 plans to kill them!

But within minutes, MC2 finds they don't have the will or capacity to kill MC1.

After such an emotional rollercoaster, MC1 is ready to turn the tables and murder MC2!

But with fated-mates this bloodthirsty, maybe they are truly made for each other.

Suggested Paranormal Genre/Subgenre: Werewolves and Shifters

Suggested Classic Romance Trope(s): Age Gap, Alpha, Enemies to Lovers, Fish-out-of-water, Forced Proximity, Marriage of Convenience.

Complimentary Romance Tropes and Paranormal Subgenres: Action and Adventure, Bully Romance, Dark Romance, Destiny, Fated Mates, Found Family, Harem/Reverse Harem, Kidnapping, Mythical Creatures, Revenge, Secret Royalty, Shape Shifters, Single Parent, Small Town, Soul Mates, Urban Fantasy, Vampires, Werewolves, Witches/Wizards, Zodiac.

NOTES:

WOLF TAMER

The Meet Cute setup: Dog trainer MC1 is used to working with cute little pooches from the film industry, not large, dominating wolves... but when captured by werewolves in need of a human to help out one of their injured pack, their knowledge of canine psychology is going to come in handy.

Can they capture the heart of the standoffish and proud alpha wolf MC2?

Suggested Paranormal Genre/Subgenre: Werewolves and Shifters

Suggested Classic Romance Trope(s): Alpha, Forced Proximity, Grumpy Sunshine, Opposites Attract.

Complimentary Romance Tropes and Paranormal Subgenres: Action and Adventure, Fated Mates, Found Family, Medical Romance, Mythical Creatures, Portal, Science-Fiction Romance, Seasonal, Shape Shifters, Superpowers, Urban Fantasy, Werewolves.

NOTES:

THEME OR SUBGENRE

~ WEREWOLVES AND VAMPIRES ~

DISAGREEING WITH DESTINY

The Meet Cute setup: In a terrible twist of fate, Werewolf MC1 discovers that Vampire MC2 is their Fated Mate!

They've never doubted destiny until now, but meeting on the battlefield and feeling that instant connection with the enemy has thrown their senses completely out of sync.

There's nothing to do but bury all feelings... But how long can a werewolf ignore its instinct?

Suggested Paranormal Genre/Subgenre: Werewolves and Shifters, Vampires

Suggested Classic Romance Trope(s): Enemies to Lovers, Opposites Attract, Romantic Suspense.

Complimentary Romance Tropes and Paranormal Subgenres: Action and Adventure, Arranged Marriage, Blind Date, Destiny, Fated Mates, Found Family, Historical, Immortals, Medieval, Monster Romance, Mythical Creatures, Regency, Revenge, Secret Royalty, Shape Shifters, Soul Mates, Time Travel, Urban Fantasy, Vampires, Werewolves.

NOTES:

THEME OR SUBGENRE
~ WEREWOLVES AND VAMPIRES ~
SECOND CHANCE PROPOSAL

The Meet Cute setup: Years ago, Star Crossed Lovers Werewolf MC1 and Vampire MC2, broke up badly due to family/pack wishes/objections after one proposed to the other.

Present day, although they won't admit it, neither has moved on. But now they are forced into a fake dating situation while they work together to project a sacred object round the clock, day and night.

Suggested Paranormal Genre/Subgenre: Werewolves and Shifters, Vampires

Suggested Classic Romance Trope(s): Celebrity, Enemies to Lovers, Fake Dating, Second Chance Romance.

Complimentary Romance Tropes and Paranormal Subgenres: Destiny, Fairytale Retelling, Fated Mates, Found Family, Historical, Immortals, Mythical Creatures, Portal, Regency, Revenge, Secret Royalty, Shape Shifters, Urban Fantasy, Vampires, Werewolves.

NOTES:

~ WITCHES/WIZARDS ~

BUYING A BROOMSTICK

The Meet Cute setup: Hardware Store Owner MC1 goes to the aid of an employee helplessly explaining that most people prefer vacuums these days, to an angry customer. The customer, Witch MC2, is in a glorious rage about the lack of broomsticks to choose from, and they are clutching an old antique-looking one with a broken handle.

MC1 interjects, trying to diffuse the situation and admires the piece of art that MC2 is holding. Luckily MC1 is an amateur woodworker who restores antique furniture in their spare time and could repair or replace the handle.

Further considerations: What other antique objects could a witch or wizard seek in the human world, and why would they be unfamiliar with modern equivalents?

Is magic acknowledged or secret? Are there magic shops and communities in your world, but none in the area MC2 has moved into? If MC2 is new in town, what is the reason for it? A dangerous plot, or something cozy and harmless like studying a new species of magical creature only found in MC1's neighborhood?

Suggested Paranormal Genre/Subgenre: Witches

Suggested Classic Romance Trope(s): Age Gap, Friends to Lovers, Grumpy Sunshine, Instalove, RomCom.

Complimentary Romance Tropes and Paranormal Subgenres: Christmas, Divine Intervention, Dragons, Fae, Fairytale Retelling, Found Family, Genie in a Bottle, Portal, Psychic Powers, Seasonal, Single Parent, Small Town, Soul Mates, Steampunk, Valentine's Day, Witches/Wizards.

NOTES:

CRASH LANDING!

The Meet Cute setup: MC1 loses control of their broomstick and crash lands into MC2's house! Was it due to uncontrollable winds during a cyclone or a faulty broomstick?

Luckily MC2 has the medical means and knowledge to patch them up. But once the bandages are on, they find themselves not wanting MC1 to leave...

Is this sudden attachment true love or some magical mayhap? Perhaps a little love potion was spilled in the crash?

How does MC2 get MC1 to stay? Do they come up with a white lie, for example, exaggerating the state of the injury, or will they simply not let MC1 go? Perhaps MC2 comes from a long line of witch hunters...

Suggested Paranormal Genre/Subgenre: Witches

Suggested Classic Romance Trope(s): Friends to Lovers, RomCom.

Complimentary Romance Tropes and Paranormal Subgenres: Academy, Action and Adventure, Christmas, Curses, Fairytale Retelling, Genie in a Bottle, Ghosts, Medical Romance, Seasonal, Single Parent, Small Town, Soul Mates, Steampunk, Urban Fantasy, Vacation, Valentine's Day, Vampires, Werewolves, Witches/Wizards, Zodiac.

NOTES:

THEME OR SUBGENRE ~ WITCHES/WIZARDS ~

DISLOYAL FAMILIAR

The Meet Cute setup: Everyone knows witches and familiars have a strong bond that can't be broken...right? So when Witch MC1's furry companion disappears, the last place they expect to find them is over at annoying neighbor MC2's house.

In typical style, the annoying human MC2 refuses to return the critter, but unexpectedly, the smug familiar is content to stay with this besotted human! But what is this apparently disloyal familiar really up to? Are they genuinely grumpy with their witch and looking to show them who's boss? Or is this matchmaking familiar just trying to give these two opposites a reason to be together?

Further considerations: Familiars can have advanced characteristics that go beyond typical animal behavior and can be supporting characters in their own right. Think, how will they communicate? Verbally or nonverbally?

Will they express themselves via body language? Or, they could have some secret and magical way of 'talking,' but only with their chosen witch or wizard? Whatever communication method you choose will have implications for the wider story, so it is a good idea to brainstorm how it might create problems or solutions before you start writing.

Suggested Paranormal Genre/Subgenre: Witches

Suggested Classic Romance Trope(s): Enemies to Lovers, Grumpy Sunshine.

Complimentary Romance Tropes & Paranormal Subgenres: Blind Date, Bounty Hunter, Christmas, Curses, Deities, Demons and Devils, Destiny, Divine Inter-vention, Dragons, Fae, Fairytale Retelling, Found Family, Ghosts, Mythical Creatures, Portal, Psychic Powers, Seasonal, Secret Royalty, Shape Shifters, Single Parent, Small Town, Urban Fantasy, Valentine's Day, Vampires, Werewolves, Witches/Wizards, Zodiac.

NOTES:

THEME OR SUBGENRE ~ WITCHES/WIZARDS ~

HALLOWEEN PARTY

The Meet Cute setup: Halloween parties go a little differently for witches and wizards. Instead of dressing up as monsters, they dress up as their favorite humans and pretend they have no magic–such a fun-filled novelty!

What happens when unlucky-in-love human MC1 accidentally crashes Witch MC2's party, who is wearing the perfect matching costume, and thinks that MC2 is their blind date!

Will MC2 usher them quickly to the door before anyone realizes there's an interloper, or will they not be able to resist pulling a few magical pranks on this hapless human, only to realize Fate is the one in control tonight.

Suggested Paranormal Genre/Subgenre: Witches

Suggested Classic Romance Trope(s): Fake Dating, Fish-out-of-water, RomCom.

Complimentary Romance Tropes and Paranormal Subgenres: Academy, Blind Date, Destiny, Divine Intervention, Dragons, Fae, Fairytale Retelling, Found Family, Seasonal, Secret Royalty, Shape Shifters, Single Parent, Small Town, Soul Mates, Vacation, Valentine's Day.

NOTES:

THEME OR SUBGENRE ~ WITCHES/WIZARDS ~

LEY WITH ME

The Meet Cute setup: Alien enthusiast MC1 is convinced that the triangulation of specific ancient historical sites is proof that aliens exist. When they stumble across Secret Witch MC2 in their search, MC2 is intrigued and amused at just how much MC1 has wrong about ley lines… and just how much they have right!

Will MC1 discover something beyond their wildest dreams? A magical community and love?

Is MC2 amused, confused or concerned at their world being discovered? Are they afraid of MC1 or for them?

Further Considerations: Beyond aliens and ley lines, what other supernatural elements could MC1 be studying, and what could they accidentally discover in the process?

Suggested Paranormal Genre/Subgenre: Witches

Suggested Classic Romance Trope(s): Fish-out-of-water, Friends to Lovers, Opposites Attract, RomCom.

Complimentary Romance Tropes and Paranormal Subgenres: Aliens, Christmas, Curses, Destiny, Divine Intervention, Found Family, GameLit, LitRPG, Mythical Creatures, Portal, Psychic Powers, Science-Fiction Romance, Seasonal, Single Parent, Small Town, Soul Mates, Urban Fantasy.Small Town.

NOTES:

OVEN COVEN

The Meet Cute setup: To build a sense of fellowship and community, the local witches coven hosts an 'Oven Coven'. A cozy cooking club where strangers are united by their shared love of baking.

Town newcomer and former big-city-chef MC1 has always excelled at baking but mistakenly assumes the 'witch' references are all to do with the upcoming Halloween and arrives in full costume–offending many of the coven. To add to this poor first impression, MC1 is embarrassed when members inform them their cookies taste terrible because they must have swapped the sugar for salt.

Fortunately, kind-hearted Single parent MC2 sprinkles a little magic and remedies the flavor but in doing so, horrifies MC1, who wasn't aware magic was real, and runs off into the night.

Suggested Paranormal Genre/Subgenre: Witches

Suggested Classic Romance Trope(s): Celebrity, Friends to Lovers, Grumpy Sunshine, RomCom.

Complimentary Romance Tropes and Paranormal Subgenres: Destiny, Divine Intervention, Dragons, Fae, Fairytale Retelling, Seasonal, Single Parent, Small Town, Soul Mates, Urban Fantasy, Valentine's Day, Witches/Wizards.

NOTES:

SCRYING MESS UP

The Meet Cute setup: Magic user MC1 is attempting to use the ancient art of scrying to find the location of a hidden treasure, but their attempts keep leading them back to human MC2.

What's going wrong? Is the spell faulty? Is MC2 wearing the object around their neck? Or could MC2 be the treasure that MC1 didn't know they were missing in their life?

Suggested Paranormal Genre/Subgenre: Witches

Suggested Classic Romance Trope(s): Age Gap, Alpha, Cinderella, Forced Proximity, Friends to Lovers, Grumpy Sunshine, Instalove, Opposites Attract.

Complimentary Romance Tropes and Paranormal Subgenres: Christmas, Curses, Destiny, Divine Intervention, Dragons, Fae, Fairytale Retelling, GameLit, Genie in a Bottle, Mythical Creatures, Seasonal, Secret Royalty, Single Parent, Small Town, Soul Mates, Steampunk, Urban Fantasy, Valentine's Day, Witches/Wizards.

NOTES:

SOUP KITCHEN CHRISTMAS

The Meet Cute setup: For centuries witches have been sharing the contents of their cauldrons with weary travelers, so it was only a matter of time before one witch decided to go all in and set up a soup kitchen.

Every December, Witch MC1's family/coven sets up a soup kitchen and over the years they have seen all sorts of people from all walks of life come through their doors, but when childhood sweetheart turned wealthy grinch MC2 arrives to shut the kitchen down, they are both about to learn the true meaning of Christmas.

Further considerations: What could have turned MC2's once open and tender heart into a cold lump of coal? Did MC1 reject them? Maybe there is an existing feud between the two families, which stretches back decades?

Furthermore, are the townsfolk aware there is magic in their midst, or does the magical community live in secret? What is the cost to either party for revealing this secret?

Suggested Paranormal Genre/Subgenre: Witches

Suggested Classic Romance Trope(s): Billionaire, Celebrity, Cinderella, Grumpy Sunshine, Second Chance Romance.

Complimentary Romance Tropes and Paranormal Subgenres: Christmas, Curses, Fairytale Retelling, Historical, Medieval, Regency, Revenge, Seasonal, Secret Baby, Secret Royalty, Shape Shifters, Single Parent, Small Town, Soul Mates, Werewolves.

NOTES:

TANGLED TAROT READING

The Meet Cute setup: MC1 has been giving Tarot readings for about as long as they can remember, when they try to read for MC2, something unusual occurs: they find their own future written in the cards. A double check in the Crystal Ball confirms their fates are entwined–and disaster is looming.

Whether for good or for ill, MC1 is convinced they need to move in together and work out what Fate has in store so they can avert disaster, but MC2 has no intention of letting anyone close to their heart, let alone allowing a stranger into their apartment.

Suggested Paranormal Genre/Subgenre: Witches

Suggested Classic Romance Trope(s): Grumpy Sunshine, Opposites Attract, Romantic Suspense, RomCom.

Complimentary Romance Tropes and Paranormal Subgenres: Christmas, Curses, Destiny, Divine Intervention, Fairytale Retelling, Found Family, GameLit, Seasonal, Secret Royalty, Shape Shifters, Single Parent, Small Town, Soul Mates, Superpowers, Urban Fantasy, Valentine's Day, Witches/Wizards.

NOTES:

THEME OR SUBGENRE ~ WITCHES/WIZARDS ~

WITCH WAY

The Meet Cute setup: Out of town, blown off course, and in need of directions, Witchy MC1 finds themself thumbing a ride for a roadside rescue. Luckily MC2 not only has a spare seat in their truck, they've got a spare room at their ranch and a heart of gold to match.

Further Considerations: What possible problems could MC2 have at their ranch that MC1 could solve? Where was MC1 on their way to, and will they want to continue to their destination, or will they decide to remain?

Suggested Paranormal Genre/Subgenre: Witches

Suggested Classic Romance Trope(s): Fish-out-of-water, Forced Proximity, Friends to Lovers.

Complimentary Romance Tropes and Paranormal Subgenres: Fairytale Retelling, Found Family, Seasonal, Single Parent, Small Town, Vacation, Valentine's Day, Witches/Wizards.

NOTES:

~ ZODIAC ~

CAT'S REVENGE

The Meet Cute setup: When the Jade Emperor, ruler of Heaven and Earth, first devised a calendar to measure time, he set up a competition for the animals to decide which creatures would get a year named after them. When Rat deceived Cat to secure better chances of winning, their friendship was betrayed.

Now, generations later, Cat's descendant MC1 has the opportunity their family has been waiting for… To assassinate the Rat heir, MC2.

But when the first pounce goes awry, will MC1 be able to hold on to their 9 lives? And how long will their game of cat and mouse last before they can admit they enjoy playing more than fighting?

Suggested Paranormal Genre/Subgenre: Fantasy Romance.

Suggested Classic Romance Trope(s): Enemies to Lovers, Instalove, Royalty,

Complimentary Romance Tropes and Paranormal Subgenres: Action and Adventure, Destiny, Fairytale Retelling, Fated Mates, GameLit, Historical, Immortals, Mythical Creatures, Portal, Revenge, Science-Fiction Romance, Seasonal, Secret Royalty, Shape Shifters, Superpowers, Urban Fantasy, Zodiac.

NOTES:

HIDDEN DRAGON

The Meet Cute setup: MC1 has never had a birthday. Their mother burned their birth certificate. Why? Because MC1 is the half-deity offspring of the Zodiac Dragon!

When MC1's powers start to develop at 18, their identity is discovered, and they are brought to the dedicated Zodiac University, where they have to resist the charms of their next-gen Zodiac classmates so they can focus on practicing their calligraphy. Then again, homework was always overrated.

Suggested Paranormal Genre/Subgenre: Fantasy Romance.

Suggested Classic Romance Trope(s): Cinderella, Enemies to Lovers, Royalty.

Complimentary Romance Tropes and Paranormal Subgenres: Academy, Bully Romance, Curses, Divine Intervention, Dragons, Fairytale Retelling, Fated Mates, GameLit, Immortals, Mythical Creatures, Portal, Revenge, Seasonal, Secret Baby, Secret Royalty, Shape Shifters, Superpowers, Zodiac.

NOTES:

INJURED TIGER

The Meet Cute setup: One of the Zodiac stories of old had the Zodiac Tiger and Monkey as good friends until the day the fearsome Tiger was caught in a trap and took a blow to their pride when Monkey came to the rescue. The exchange secured Monkey's spot on the Zodiac calendar, but Tiger lived resentfully forever after.

It's understandable when modern-day MC1 comes to the rescue of injured Tiger MC2, MC2 is cagey and distrustful.

Will MC1 be able to prove they want nothing in return? Maybe MC1 will be the balm to the anger that has kept Tiger pride smoldering for thousands of years...

Suggested Paranormal Genre/Subgenre: Fantasy Romance.

Suggested Classic Romance Trope(s): Enemies to Lovers.

Complimentary Romance Tropes and Paranormal Subgenres: Action and Adventure, Destiny, Divine Intervention, Fairytale Retelling, Fated Mates, GameLit, Immortals, Kidnapping, LitRPG, Mythical Creatures, Portal, Psychic Powers, Seasonal, Secret Royalty, Shape Shifters, Soul Mates, Superpowers, Zodiac.

NOTES:

KIDNAPPED ZODIAC SPOUSE

The Meet Cute setup: Human MC1 is selected, abducted and delivered, to be the new spouse of Zodiac MC2, who is about to find out they got more than they bargained for.

Kidnapping a bride? What century does MC2 think they're living in? MC1 is sure to teach them a thing or two about modern values!

Suggested Paranormal Genre/Subgenre: Fantasy Romance.

Suggested Classic Romance Trope(s): Age Gap, Alpha, Forced Proximity, Royalty.

Complimentary Romance Tropes and Paranormal Subgenres: Arranged Marriage, Dark Romance, Immortals, Kidnapping, Monster Romance, Mythical Creatures, Portal, Superpowers, Urban Fantasy, Zodiac.

NOTES:

MISTAKEN ZODIAC

The Meet Cute setup: MC1 is a messenger from the gods on a mission to fetch the new incarnation of a Zodiac guardian, a human who will step up and take their place with the other Zodiac.

When MC2 is told of their destiny, they're thrilled...but when their powers fail to manifest, everyone begins to question if MC1 got it wrong.

With MC1's job and the balance of the universe at stake, will MC2 be able to fake it until they make it? Or will they mess things up further by falling in love in the process?

Suggested Paranormal Genre/Subgenre: Fantasy Romance.

Suggested Classic Romance Trope(s): Cinderella, Fish-out-of-water.

Complimentary Romance Tropes and Paranormal Subgenres: Academy, Curses, Deities, Destiny, Divine Intervention, Fairytale Retelling, Found Family, GameLit, Genie in a Bottle, Immortals, Kidnapping, LitRPG, Mythical Creatures, Psychic Powers, Superpowers, Urban Fantasy, Zodiac.

NOTES:

PARANORMAL MATCHMAKER

The Meet Cute setup: Unlucky in love, MC1 goes to a matchmaker who is also a fortune teller, hoping if they give the task of picking their next suitor to a professional, the relationship won't end in a train wreck like all their last attempts.

Unfortunately, this matchmaking medium uses their paranormal ability to irrevocably tie MC1's future with a suitor before checking with them! What happens when the destiny cord attaches MC1 to someone they deem totally unsuitable?

A high school rival? Long-term enemy? Teacher or boss? Best friend's boyfriend? On their journey to untie this cosmic tangle, they might just spark a fire that can't be put out...

Suggested Paranormal Genre/Subgenre: Fantasy Romance.

Suggested Classic Romance Trope(s): Age Gap, Enemies to Lovers, Fake Dating, Fish-out-of-water, Forced Proximity, Friends to Lovers, Grumpy Sunshine, Opposites Attract, Romcom.

Complimentary Romance Tropes and Paranormal Subgenres: Academy, Blind Date, Christmas, Curses, Destiny, Divine Intervention, Fairytale Retelling, Fated Mates, Genie in a Bottle, Mafia, Mythical Creatures, Secret Royalty, Shape Shifters, Single Parent, Small Town, Superpowers, Zodiac.

NOTES:

POWERLESS ZODIAC GUARDIAN

The Meet Cute setup: Zodiac Guardian MC1 has been injured and or attacked, and had the source of their power stolen–meaning they can no longer protect the balance of the universe!

Luckily, human MC2 finds them and nurses them back to health. As they regain their strength, MC1 falls hard for their human 'guardian angel' while MC2 starts to believe the fantastical things MC1 has been rambling in their sleep might not just be due to the drugs...

Suggested Paranormal Genre/Subgenre: Fantasy Romance.

Suggested Classic Romance Trope(s): Forced Proximity, Friends to Lovers.

Complimentary Romance Tropes and Paranormal Subgenres: Destiny, Divine Intervention, Dragons, Fae, Fairytale Retelling, Found Family, Medical Romance, Mythical Creatures, Portal, Psychic Powers, Single Parent, Small Town, Soul Mates, Superpowers, Zodiac.

NOTES:

ZODIAC HEIR

The Meet Cute setup: When every generation of the Zodiac dies, they are replaced with a human descendant of the original Zodiac royalty, born under the correct signs and conditions.

When MC1 is taken, rescued some might say, from their dead-end job and piling up debt to become the new Zodiac sign, they jump at the chance to do something extraordinary.

But when they meet the other Zodiacs, all devilishly handsome and full of trouble, they realize it will take hard work to claim their proper place and not be dominated by the other signs' powerful personalities.

Further considerations: What sign is your MC? How will this impact their relationships with the others? Are you going to make this a Reverse Harem story or a series with a different original MC for every Zodiac?

Suggested Paranormal Genre/Subgenre: Fantasy Romance.

Suggested Classic Romance Trope(s): Cinderella, Enemies to Lovers, Fish-out-of-water, Forced Proximity, Friends to Lovers.

Complimentary Romance Tropes and Paranormal Subgenres: Academy, Bully Romance, Fated Mates, Found Family, GameLit, Harem/Reverse Harem, Immortals, Mythical Creatures, Portal, Psychic Powers, Secret Royalty, Shape Shifters, Zodiac.

NOTES:

ZODIAC MILITARY

The Meet Cute setup: The Zodiac are a super secret branch of the military consisting of twelve brothers-in-arms, each possessing the power of one of the signs of the zodiac.

After a previous mission went terribly wrong, Zodiac MC1 decides they should call it quits... They take one final mission to protect MC2 and fall head over heels for their client.

Will MC2 help them fix their failing confidence?

Suggested Paranormal Genre/Subgenre: Fantasy Romance.

Suggested Classic Romance Trope(s): Bodyguard/Military, Celebrity, Cinderella, Instalove, Marriage of Convenience, Opposites Attract, Romantic Suspense, RomCom, Royalty.

Complimentary Romance Tropes and Paranormal Subgenres: Academy, Action and Adventure, Fated Mates, Found Family, GameLit, Harem/Reverse Harem, Immortals, LitRPG, Mythical Creatures, Portal, Psychic Powers, Secret Royalty, Shape Shifters, Superpowers, Time Travel, Urban Fantasy, Zodiac.

NOTES:

~ WRITING CRAFT SECTION ~
UNDERSTANDING THE MEET-CUTE

Why the First Meeting is So Important.

The term ***Meet-cute*** was originally a cinematic term to describe the scene in a film when the two main protagonists, destined to be a couple by the end, meet for the *first* time.

Typically this first meeting had to be memorable to get the Viewer to 'pay attention' and signal the importance of these two people in terms of the plot. Because a lot of films with romantic themes were romantic comedies, or at least used elements of humor, the first meeting would often be sweet, funny, or—*you guessed it*—cute.

Thus Meet-cute became the shorthand term to reference a couple's first meeting—regardless of whether the meeting was cute or funny—and the term has since been co-opted by writers of novels, short stories, and plays.

Arguably, the Meet-Cute is the most important event in a romantic story.

Why? Because, in story-crafting language, the Meet-cute is *a romantic **inciting incident:*** a catalyst event whereby two people's lives are *irrevocably changed* because the other person enters their life.

~ WRITING CRAFT SECTION ~

Meet-cutes are a crucial element for character and plot developments, but just as important: for hooking the Reader. **This is because the meet-cute *sets the scene*** establishing the tone and genre of the story. And this insight should indicate to the Reader whether it's the kind of story they will enjoy. Ultimately it is the meet-cute's 'job' to convince the Reader to come along on the story journey.

What should a Meet-cute actually do?

A well-crafted Meet-cute should ***showcase the main characters' personalities*** as they exist now, prior to meeting the person that will change them and make their lives better. The Reader should think to themselves: these two people are meant to be together, even if (*especially if!*) the characters completely disagree.

Also, the Meet-cute should be ***true to the overall tone*** **of the rest of the story**.

For example if you're writing using the romance trope of RomCom then the tone of the Meet-cute also needs to be comedic—perhaps setting up a misunderstanding or a lie. But if your story has a 'darker' tone, like Mafia, or Romantic suspense, then the Meet-cute should likewise be tense and dramatic rather than sweet or light-hearted.

NOTES:

GLOSSARY OF CLASSIC ROMANCE TROPES

Age Gap

Trope Definition: *Age Gap* is a shorthand way of noting that one of the characters is not only older but *significantly* older than their partner–or destined to be their partner —by at least ten to fifteen years or more.

Traditionally, the male is the elder of the pairing. Flipping this around is possible, but be mindful of Reader expectations if your goal is to create a commercial product.

In real life, you may have heard of such a relationship referred to as a *May to December* relationship, although this term is more common in the UK rather than the USA.

Alpha

Trope Definition: Coming from a paranormal romance writer's perspective, you may assume that an Alpha refers to the leader of a werewolf clan. And while that is true, in a *broader* romance context across all romance subgenres, whether paranormal, contemporary or historical, an Alpha is a gender specific term referring to *any* domineering male.

Typically, the *Alpha Trope* refers to *any entitled type* who believes they are number one. A common set up is they have been born into wealth or power and have been raised to think they are naturally better than other people. With this attitude and mindset firmly entrenched, the Alpha character will try to dominate or bully their destined partner.

Fortunately, through the power of love, and by learning a few hard truths along the way, they discover the error of their ways, overcome those characteristics, and so by the end of the book they acknowledge their partner as their *equal*.

GLOSSARY OF CLASSIC ROMANCE TROPES

Billionaire

Trope Definition: The clue is in the name, this trope involves a character (almost always a man) and guess what? They are *uber*-rich.

Whether they were born into the wealthy elite, are self-made business entrepreneurs, or have inherited their wealth depends on the sub-genre.

The *Billionaire trope* works very well with the *Alpha trope* as your Billionaire may be *spoiled* in the beginning of the story, and it's only the love interest who can show them there is more to life than money.

Bodyguard, and Military

Trope Definition: While this trope can refer to someone actually employed as a Bodyguard, it can also be a shorthand to attribute someone with protective feelings or an obligation to protect or provide protection to another. Typically this protection is physical.

Similar to the *Bodyguard* trope, is the Military trope. Something all these tropes have in common is their protagonists are highly skilled individuals who have been professionally trained to fight, hand to hand combat, close quarter weapons, and so on.

In its traditional form, an individual employed in a bodyguard role, the source of conflict at the heart of this trope is where the professional work ethic crosses over into personal territory. Protecting their assigned person becomes a personal responsibility directly tied to their inner emotional happiness as romantic feelings develop for their charge. A great deal of time may be spent with the bodyguard denying those very unprofessional feelings.

Depending on whether this is a Bodyguard or a Military trope, the protagonist may or may not work well in teams. Often Bodyguards are 'loners' and independent thinkers, whereas those with a military background *work well* in teams.

However, military-trained operatives often find themselves frustrated when forced to deal with civilians who lack any formal training and can't follow simple rules. Pairing a rule-loving military type with a love interest who has an opposing view on the value or necessity of following rules, especially for their own safety, will create fun character conflicts that can serve as an underlying tone to stack behind larger plot conflicts and story obstacles.

Celebrity

Trope Definition: A *Celebrity trope* often focuses on the *power disparity* between a couple as its central source of conflict.

Much like rich and poor, the famous and the nobodies are seen as a class divide that shall not mix. Celebrities come in all shapes and sizes and in varying degrees of fame, from local to international. What sets the famous apart from regular folks is that they need no introduction to the people around them, who inevitably want to hang out with these living legends.

Another core source of conflict that this trope can utilize is how the Celebrity handles their fame. Do they love it or hate it? Whatever you choose, making the love interest *think the opposite* will establish a core personality conflict that must be resolved by the end of the story if these two are to become a perfect match.

Cinderella

Trope Definition: Less about the original fairytale, *Cinderella* is a shorthand or encompassing term for a story where there is a rags-to-riches reversal.

A *Cinderella trope* traditionally involves a hardworking and poor person whose daily life struggles are about to vanish upon meeting their handsome prince, or at least their Billionaire, Royal, and or Celebrity.

Money, and lack thereof, is the core conflict, playing upon the time-worn divide of social classes where the Cinderella character worries they aren't good enough for the love interest, or they are told they aren't good enough by antagonistic third parties.

Despite being an extremely old-fashioned idea, this conflict still works in a modern setting if the couple have money and class hang-ups.

Enemies to Lovers

Trope Definition: *Enemies to Lovers* is a time-honored trope that remains popular because the conflict is built-in and core to the relationship from the start.

The prospective couple may be genuine enemies, on opposing sides of a military conflict or gang war. They may come from feuding families, in the tradition of Romeo and Juliet. Or they may simply work for opposite businesses and actually be *rivals* rather than true enemies.

Generally, an 'enemy' in the modern sense wants the same objective as their rival, but there's only one of whatever it is up for grabs, for example, a valuable artwork or even a job promotion. It doesn't have to be a tangible item, it could be 'a win' of some kind. For example, the coach of a rival team is an enemy because only one team can win the season.

Sometimes the enemy wants the same goal but for very different reasons. What they consider 'a win' may mean the destruction of their counterpart's goal. For example, a person wanting to keep a dog shelter open would be the natural enemy of a land developer who wants to profit from the sale of the land the shelter is renting.

A word of caution: While in the beginning, the couple may have an active dislike of their counterpart, it needs to be quickly established that they have respect for their rival even if they can't let anyone know. Don't make the mistake of creating an enemy who has fundamentally opposite values or is incompatible on an ethical level. While the characters should "love to hate" each other on an *external* level, they must not be repulsed or disgusted by the other's internal behavior and personality.

Fake Dating

Trope Definition: Two people enter into an agreement to *publicly* appear as a couple or in a relationship of some kind, while in truth, both parties are fully aware that this relationship is false and they have no romantic feelings for the other.

For example, posing as a date to a wedding or being a girlfriend over the summer. Usually, the arrangement is to trick or fool a third party, whether to merely save face or for financial gain. Typically, one-half of the fake couple has *significantly more* to lose if their arrangement is revealed to be false, and this looming threat is the initial source of the conflict.

Often, the partner in the fake couple will be a friend wanting to help out, but equally, they may have an agenda of their own and plan to exploit the person desperate to appear to be in a relationship.

The main difference between *Fake Dating* and its similar trope, *Marriage of Convenience*, is the legal aspect and proposed duration. A *Marriage of Convenience* arrangement is a legally binding and usually long-term relationship. *Fake Dating* is theoretically a short, non-binding agreement. We say theoretically because naturally, the couple fall in love and the temporary union becomes permanent...

Fish-out-of-water

Trope Definition: This is both a *situational* and a *personality/character-*based trope whereby an individual is put into a setting they are not equipped to handle, most often because the new environment is opposite to their personal experiences or emotional capacity up to this point. For example, a fast-living big city type is stranded in a quiet small town.

The Fish-out-of-water trope is often the backbone of many comedies, particularly RomCom, because a character struggling to cope in a 'foreign' environment naturally lends itself to a clash of cultures in surprising, and therefore funny, juxtapositions. For example, an elite military officer used to barking orders suddenly has to deal with a bunch of uncooperative toddlers.

However, this trope can be used in serious situations too. The key to toning down the comedy angle is to remember that this character *isn't* incompetent, but rather their particular skills and knowledge are opposite of where they find themselves. Furthermore, adding an emotional subtext that is equal to, or greater, than the clash of cultures will reduce the humor. For example, with our elite officer, if the school room is populated by older children who are overcoming their own challenges, then while the premise remains the same: the children won't do what the officer wants, the emotion has changed from one of comedic chaos to one of striving for independence.

Forced Proximity

Trope Definition: A couple finds themselves stuck together, literally or figuratively, whether they like it, or not. And commonly, in the beginning, they *do not* enjoy or want to be stuck with the other party, hence the 'forced' part of the trope.

Theoretically, in a forced proximity trope, *neither party can walk away from the situation*. While this trope is often initiated through the physical setting, for example, trapped in an elevator overnight, it can also be due to the character's personality and emotional situation. For example, being stuck in a job when there are pressing bills to pay and little opportunity for other employment would qualify, but keep in mind, *from the reader's perspective* the 'more stuck together' the couple are, the better.

One of the great strengths of this trope is that it lends itself equally well to comedic or suspenseful situations.

Friends to Lovers

Trope Definition: Most commonly, when planning to use this trope, the prospective couple should already be friends, or at least know each other in some capacity. And often, especially if they are very good friends, there's a strong possibility that one has been in love with the other for some time. They might or might not be aware of this attraction, but most likely they will be denying their feelings, or labeling them as hopeless or inappropriate. If they don't already have a feeling of attraction, these feelings can be awakened when suddenly seeing their acquaintance in a new light, for example, perhaps the acquaintance returns after a time away.

Very often, the conflict at the heart of this pairing is from one or both of the friends being afraid of ruining the relationship they already have and/or breaking social taboos which will lead to rejection. This can depend on a person's perception of how high the risk is. Many people are afraid to act if the consequences could result in a complete loss of a person's company, something they consider would make them more miserable than living with their unrequited love.

Grumpy Sunshine

Trope Definition: *Grumpy Sunshine* is a quick term, basically, it's a summary of the two defining personality types. One person is known as being the 'grumpy' character and the other has a *sunny* disposition.

The reason it works is this pairing is a classic example of *Opposites Attract.*

It is *extremely* common, almost to the point it's a rule, that the man will be the 'grumpy' one. What exactly makes them this way is where you're free to decide, and they don't literally have to be angry or upset all the time. They may simply be a strict rule follower, which makes them appear as up-tight, or by the book, or even proud.

What's more, this grumpy demeanor is not typically how they view themselves, but rather how the 'sunshine' personality views them. And it's often that interaction with the sunshine character that causes the upset or *exasperates* the 'grumpy' person.

Because, remember, this trope is essentially opposites attract. So perhaps the 'sunny' character may have a more relaxed view of whatever rules that Mr Grumpy strictly adheres to.

Just keep in mind that the 'grumpy' one's behavior ***should not*** focus on being outrightly *mean to the other person.* Also, while often the ***sunshine*** character is portrayed as being naive, that isn't necessary, often they can just be very open, and have a bubbly personality–while their opposite, the grumpy to their sunshine, is a closed-off person with a reserved personality.

Instalove

Trope Definition: Unlike most romances where love between the characters develops and blooms over the course of the narrative, an *Instalove* trope is when, you guessed it, the soon-to-be-a-couple falls head over heels for each other *the instant* they set eyes on the other.

Put aside any doubts you may have that this concept is a bit over the top because *Instalove* isn't meant to portray real life, and it's the escapist quality of this larger-than-life set-up that is what devoted Readers are looking for.

In a paranormal context, *Instalove* works especially well for soul mate or fated-fates themes and is often used in werewolf stories, but it's not limited to just that sub-genre.

The *Instalove* trope is a handy plot device to move along or speed up any plot and is especially useful when you might be looking to cut down on pages and word counts if, for example, you were writing a short story. Indeed, *Instalove* is a tried and true convenient used in many short reads, so lean into the trope if you want to target the romance reader market who are after a quick 'hit' of love.

Marriage of Convenience

Trope Definition: The main difference between this trope from its cousin, the *Fake Dating* trope is, in a *Marriage of Convenience*, this is a *real* and legally binding situation. Unlike Fake Dating, the couple are not *feigning* to be married.

Most often, *both parties* should have something to gain, some greater goal they are after, otherwise, why do it? And so whatever that gain/goal is, part of the conditions to acquire it, means that they *must* get married. Often the gain/goal is an inheritance of some kind.

For either *Marriage of Convenience* or *Fake Dating* the couple can be total strangers, or acquaintances. While the two parties may enter into the agreement without any romantic feelings for each other if they do know each other already, then this trope pairs very nicely with the trope *Friends to Lovers*, and if you think about the aspect of agreeing to the marriage to 'gain' something, if one of the pair is already secretly in love–by accepting the offer of marriage what they hope to gain is the opportunity, or courage, to confess their true affection for their love-interest.

Opposites Attract

Trope Definition: In many ways, 'opposites attract' is the basis for the majority of romance stories. Contrary to real life, where being partnered with your true opposite would most likely result in chaos rather than harmony, by utilizing this trope in fiction, and especially in romance, you can create an astonishingly satisfying experience for the reader.

Why does this trope work so well?

The rules of fiction denote that wherever there is *opposition* there is *conflict*, and the *more* conflict you can pack into the story, the *more* your readers will be absolutely dying to find out how this situation will be resolved. How will you the writer make these two incomplete opposites realize that by being together they create one perfect whole? The more perfectly you wrap up seemingly impossible situations, the more your reader will feel that you have given them a complete and satisfying story, because opposition turned into unity creates harmony.

So, where to start? It's fairly easy to start broadly, if MC1 is rich, then

MC2 is poor.

And while in paranormal romance there are some well-established 'oppositions' some can be misleading, for example, werewolves versus vampires are just enemies rather than true opposites. Whereas, a human paired with a vampire is their opposite if you consider their seemingly incompatible lifespans.

Rather than starting with enemies, to find opposites delve into mindsets and attitudes. *Archetypal characters* make for great foundations when applying an opposites attract rule.

Angels and Devils (While in paranormal romance this can be literal, on a mindset level it's more about Do-gooders being the opposites of Evil-doers)

- Cops and Thieves (Law-abiding versus outlaws)
- Environmentalists and Developers (Selfless versus selfish)
- Creatives and Critics (self-expression versus censor)
- Hard-working/responsible versus Carefree/irresponsible
- Worldly types versus the innocent.
- Jaded or cynical versus Open-hearted (often called a "Grumpy/ Sunshine" relationship).

Romantic Suspense

Trope Definition: Not only is *Romantic Suspense a* trope, it's also an extremely popular sub-genre within itself, especially in contemporary romance where you will find many 'woman in danger/abduction' based plots.

The *Romantic Suspense* trope revolves around the core issue of trust. For example, MC1 falls for their MC2, but the catch is that MC1 *doesn't know* if they can *entirely trust* MC2, and this goes deeper than a feeling, plot elements can be drawn from the mystery or thriller genres, for example, a character afraid that their shady past will catch up with them, or becoming entangled with a present-day crime.

Adding a layer of paranormal can really ramp up the dramatic tension. It is one thing for a regular character to wonder if they can trust an ex-con for example, but make that person a vampire, and well then, the issues of life and death become a reality.

Quite often in *Romantic Suspense,* whether a trope or genre, your MC1 will already have aspects of danger within their lives–maybe they are a criminal, or associated with the wrong side of the law. The tension between external dangers and internal suspense, such as wondering if MC2 is *who they say they are*, should keep the reader on the edge of their seat until the very end when all is resolved.

RomCom

Trope Definition: *RomCom* is an abbreviation of 'Romantic Comedy,' so it should come as no surprise that this trope focuses on humor as its core defining and unifying element.

The meet-cute itself should reflect this humor, and typically the meeting of the two may involve some form of physical humor–they bump, they spill coffee, they get in the wrong car, they switch bags unwittingly, etc. But it also often revolves around whacky, or over-the-top miscommunications, false assumptions or outright lies that form the basis of the crazy situation the MCs have suddenly landed themselves in.

RomComs have, since their inception, remained lighthearted in tone and should never venture into *truly* dark themes. Readers are looking for fun, *escapist* fiction, not horrifying nightmarish situations or grim moral quandaries–while your characters may face mortal peril, lean into situations with an element of absurdity or tongue in cheek. If they're about to get killed then the method of execution might be a *looming* threat of something nasty rather than actual terror as rats gnaw on their faces.

However, while the underlying themes remain on the lighter side of life, RomComs can be anywhere on the 'heat' scale, with sexual activity ranging from sweet/clean to steamy.

Royalty / Social Elite

Trope Definition: One or possibly both of the MCs are royals–or 'royal adjacent'–think members of some elite portion of their society. So, for example, through a paranormal lens, this could be the Alpha in a werewolf Clan. Whatever type of social elite your MC is, this trope comes into play when it's their position at the top of the hierarchy which is creating the complications in their life.

A common variant is the 'secret' royal trope, rather than being open with their position, in this subversion, our royal MC is posing as a regular person for whatever reason. So think carefully about the setup, why would your MC pose as just one of the faceless masses when they could be worshiped? A good place to start if you want to create a core conflict from this trope, or any of its related tropes Celebrity, Billionaire, Cinderella, simply brainstorm this premise: what might be the cost of living in a gilded cage?

While most of us have little idea of how royals actually live, in our modern age of celebrity we can make some fair astute guesses when everyone knows who 'you are', bringing a paradoxical mix of freedom through privilege *and* yet restriction due to that immediate recognition. You have money, but if you can't go out and spend it without being swamped by strangers... You get the idea.

And speaking of spending all that lovely life-changing cash, the Royal/ Elite trope is an intriguing concept for the reader, playing on an assumed universal fantasy of the joy of being born into wealth and power. Readers tend to be fascinated by the privilege, and want to be immersed in complex worlds with lush descriptions.

Second Chance Romance

Trope Definition: The MCs in your story have been romantically involved in their pasts, or at the very least, know each other from years ago. If they weren't an actual couple then it's likely that one had a crush on the other, generally, there should have been *some* attraction. For whatever reason these two didn't stay together, most often their relationship simply didn't work out, or they were separated for reasons beyond their control.

But now, life, the universe and everything has put them back together, and as the trope's name suggests they get a 'second chance' at their romantic relationship.

This is a delightful trope, and it can be applied to pretty much any paranormal romance. Furthermore, if you like coming up with a complete backstory for your characters, then Second Chance Romance is a great way to make use of all that research and backstory.

Do take the time to brainstorm why this pair didn't make it the first time they were in each other's lives because it's those reasons that will help generate the conflict for why they might think it's also not going to work out this time either.

Here are four basic questions to get the ideas flowing, ask yourself:

How long ago **they were a couple?** This can be useful for establishing tone, because for example, the tender love of childhood sweethearts creates a different vibe than a drunken one-night fling in their college years.

How *serious* was the relationship at the time? Were they both in love? Was one secretly in love? Was it first love? Were they married?

Next, brainstorm, ***why didn't* it work out back then?** Work commitments? Career ambitions? They moved towns? Did a third party force them apart?

Finally, have a think about each MC's current *emotional* state. **How do they *feel* about the other person now?**

Do they actively loathe them? Do they just think that 'trying again' is a pointless waste of time because it's *doomed* to fail. After all, crush my heart once, shame on me, crush my heart twice...

Then again, maybe one of them has been *waiting their whole life* to remedy the regret of letting that person go?

NOTES:

BONUS AMPLIFIER QUESTIONS

If you find yourself stuck, or maybe you have an idea, but it's not quite right, then to help you tweak and spark more ideas for each of the meet-cutes we have provided, just ask yourself these questions: (in no particular order).

- **Who has the most to lose?** Is the Point of View character the one with the most to lose in this scene? If not, will switching the protagonist's Point of View work better?
- **Timing.** What if one of the characters entered this scene five minutes later or earlier? What would have changed in that time?
- **Story Tone.** Is the meet-cute set-up complementary and true to the underlying tone in general?
- **Secrets.** Keeping a secret is an intriguing way to start a story, but a potentially fraught way to start a romantic relationship. What secret could one character have? What could happen if it were exposed?
- **The bad day gets worse.** What if your protagonist was already having one of the worst days of their life? How does meeting their counterpart ***make it worse***?
- **Mistaken identity** is a fun complication to add that works equally well for comedic or dramatic purposes. What if one of the characters wasn't who they say they are, or, are mistakenly assumed to be someone else? How far down the path of their relationship will this false identity carry on?
- **Sales.** One of them is trying to sell something to the other. What could it be?
- **Change the Location.** A seemingly simple detail, but one that can have dramatic effects. Where does the current meet-cute take place? List five to ten possible alternatives, taking into

consideration cities and countries, but also venues. Some examples: Cafe, motel, hotel, beach, theme park, college, museum, archives, science lab, holding cell, car park, mall, polling station, rally, sport events, music concert, rehearsal-wedding, play, award ceremony. Now, are these venues modern? Or old and run-down? Who owns them? Why are they here? Is it dangerous to be here?

- **Have they met before?** What if your characters actually met for the first time last night? What happened? Do they recognise each other at the official meet-cute, or not? Why not? Is one lying? Why?

- **Family relationships.** What is one, or both, are **single parents**? Does being a parent give them *more or less in common* with their counterpart at the point of meet-cute?

- **Vacation.** What if one was on vacation. Why did they come here? How does the temporary location affect their inhibitions?

- **Dropped object.** What if one sees the other drop something. What is it? Do they try to return it? Or flip the idea–what if the other comes up to your protagonist, claiming they dropped an object. What is it? Is it valuable? Is it connected to an appointment or a secret they are trying to keep? Do they claim the item or deny recognising it?

- **Grass is greener.** What is it about your protagonist that they wish they could change? How does their meet-cute counterpart represent that longing?

NOTES:

Thank You!

& A Small Request...

Thank you so much for reading this collection of Meet Cutes and we hope it has sparked many Romance Stories Ideas. If you could **please post a review** on Amazon or Goodreads, we would really appreciate it.

All the best, Love,
King & Carpenter.

If you enjoyed this Book, you might also like:

Meet Cute Story Ideas for Contemporary Romance

Softcover – 978-0-473-65865-6

ebook – 978-0-473-65867-0

Made in the USA
Las Vegas, NV
04 January 2026

38550669R00109